FURTWÄNGLER

Furtwängler

Hans-Hubert Schönzeler

Foreword by
Sir Yehudi Menuhin, O.M.

Duckworth

First published in 1990 by
Gerald Duckworth & Co Ltd.
The Old Piano Factory
43 Gloucester Crescent, London NW1

ISBN 0 7156 2313 5

British Library Cataloguing in Publication Data

Schönzeler, Hans-Hubert *1925–*
    Furtwängler.
    1. Music. Conducting. Furtwängler, Wilhelm, 1886–1954
    I. Title
    785′.092′4

    ISBN 0-7156-2313-3

Photoset in North Wales by
Derek Doyle & Associates, Mold, Clwyd
Printed in Great Britain by
Redwood Press Ltd, Melksham, Wiltshire

Contents

Foreword

by Sir Yehudi Menuhin, O.M.

Furtwängler has become almost a cult figure: a voice from history evoking a conception of life and music at odds with today's calculated distress – a last voice from a romantic age when time was yet fluid and discreet. Microseconds, count-down to the next disaster, the pressure of deadlines – the very subtractings of time from itself that we now practise – all these have transformed time itself from a benevolent ground-tone to a jealous, menacing taskmaster. Furtwängler mastered time; time served *him*. He used time for making music and for helping musicians to escape from Nazi Germany. He spent time reading and contemplating, aware that the cultivation and worship of beauty were the supreme things in life. It was a rearguard action indeed in Nazi Germany.

Once, when rehearsing in occupied Berlin in a makeshift cinema, I heard the voice of despair. A *cri de coeur* broke from Furtwängler's lips: 'Wo ist *mein* Deutschland?' – 'Where is *my* Germany?' His recordings and the memory of his manner, his appearance and his conducting have bequeathed us echoes of *his* Germany, *his* Beethoven, *his* Brahms.

Preface

I stem from a Leipzig family. Both my parents were amateur musicians and were passionately interested in music. My mother heard Nikisch concerts in the *Gewandhaus*, and in 1922 was present when Furtwängler conducted the memorial concert for Nikisch. In 1928 she heard the boy Yehudi Menuhin give his first recital there, and ever after the names of Nikisch, Furtwängler and Menuhin were our *lares et penates*.

I began to learn the violin at five or six, and when I was about eight my mother took me to my first concert at the *Gewandhaus*. Not the concert proper, for it was virtually impossible to get seats, but on Thursday morning there was the so-called 'General Public Rehearsal' which in fact was a preview of the evening concert. I cannot remember the programme, but I seem to recollect that it contained some Schubert. What I do remember vividly is that I came out with tears streaming down my face and stated flatly to my mother: '*Mutti*, I am going to become a conductor.' Her answer was highly uncomplimentary – to the effect that I was crazy. Looking back, I feel she was pretty nearly right.

Through circumstances political and otherwise, I did not have another chance of hearing Furtwängler until after my emigration and in an Australian internment camp. There we had Furtwängler's famous recording of Tchaikovsky's *Pathétique* Symphony which he had made in 1938, and it overwhelmed me. My teacher, Dr Georg Gruber, a former conductor of the Vienna Boys' Choir, calmly said to me: 'The great impression you have just had was 50 per cent Tchaikovsky and 50 per cent Furtwängler!'

After the war came my years of study at the Sydney Conservatorium. I tried to listen to as many Furtwängler recordings as I could in the immediate post-war years in Australia, and my admiration grew steadily. Then, in 1950, I came to Europe and settled in London, and the great day came on 22 May: Furtwängler conducted the Philharmonia (in a programme, incidentally, which included Kirsten Flagstadt singing the first performance of Strauss's 'Four Last Songs'). I somehow got permission to attend the final rehearsal and had my first chance of meeting Furtwängler personally. He was most kind, and patiently listened to my story, more or less as I have told it here.

I have often been asked whether I was a personal friend of Furtwängler's. Unfortunately I must say no, for he had few friends outside his own close circle. But he always remembered me, and I could go to all his rehearsals and come to him with my own musical problems. As he was a fairly regular guest in London we met quite frequently in rehearsals and after concerts, and the kindness and understanding he showed me at our first meeting remained unaltered. Also he never stinted his advice to young 'colleagues' like myself.

Both as a man and as a musician he was great and modest at all times. I admired and adored him, and I am grateful to have the chance of writing this biography. Much has been written about the artist, and as much about his political involvements, but far too little about the man and his complex personality, though that revolves entirely round his music. We must therefore look at the man and his life first and foremost. He himself once stated that his biographer would have to be someone who was both a musician and a writer. It is my foolish hope that, in writing this book, I fulfil these stipulations.

I am grateful for the assistance given me by the archivists of the following institutions: Bibliothèque et Musée de l'Opéra (Paris); Ministère des Affaires Etrangères, Service du Protocole (Paris); New York Philharmonic; Salzburger Festspiele; Wilhelm Furtwängler Society (UK); Zentralbibliothek Zürich (Musikabteilung). My sincerest thanks go to Frau Elisabeth Furtwängler for her generous help and hospitality, and to Patrick B. Allen, Dr Günter Birkner, John Braun, Hans Gál, Dr Mireille Geering, Hans Geiger, Andrew Guyatt, Colin Haycraft, John Hunt, Hans

Keller and Yehudi Menuhin. Last but not least, I am grateful to my wife Helmi, who has helped me with this book in every way.

All pictorial material was kindly put at my disposal by Frau Elisabeth Furtwängler out of the Furtwängler Archive, Clarens. Where the photographs are professional and the source is known, this is shown in brackets after the captions.

H.H. Sch.

1

Background

The greatness of a great man cannot be explained simply by heredity: there are too many other factors, mainly of an indefinable, spiritual nature which have a larger and more important bearing on his genius. Nevertheless it is not without interest to look at the roots, at the ancestry of such a person, since naturally they also have their formative effects.

The Furtwängler family stems from the heart of the Black Forest and, according to the researches of Herzfeld, goes back to the thirteenth or fourteenth century.[1] The Furtwängler home was a farmhouse in true Black Forest style with a steep sloping roof and low hanging eaves which stands to this day, though it now no longer belongs to the family. It is situated in the region around the small town of Furtwangen, some fifteen miles east of Freiburg, and was affectionately known as the 'Furtwängle'. For many generations the Furtwänglers were farmers and only married within their own area. Furtwängler therefore, on his paternal side, was a man who sprang basically from South German peasant stock. This may at one and the same time explain his innate stubbornness and his close contact with all that is in nature and related to God-given growth.

Until the early nineteenth century the Furtwänglers were bound to the soil. They then turned away from the land and became artisans, and a few emigrated, so that Wilhelm Furtwängler could say, much later: 'Wherever I go, I seem to

---

[1] In order not to clutter up the text unduly, I shall in this instance and in the following simply refer to Herzfeld, Höcker, Riess, etc. Details of these works which I have drawn on for information can be found in 'Recommended Reading'.

meet namesakes of mine.' Those who remained in their home region turned mostly to watchmaking, and it is perhaps of whimsical interest to note that one of these ancestors, in 1868, founded a small factory where he manufactured cuckoo-clocks with Westminster chimes.

The first Furtwängler to break with the rural surroundings was another Wilhelm – the conductor's grandfather. He went to high school in Freiburg, studied theology and finally archaeology, and was an ardent student of Greek culture. But after two years' travel in Greece he failed to find a living in his chosen subject, and became a teacher, ending up as headmaster of a high school in Freiburg. His son Adolf (1853-1907) was to become one of the founders of modern Greek studies. He attended the universities of Freiburg, Leipzig and Munich and first attracted attention during the excavations at Olympia. In 1884 he was called to Berlin, and ten years later became Professor of Archaeology and director of three museums and collections in Munich. The same year he married Adelheid Wendt (1863-1944).

In contrast to the Furtwänglers, the Wendts were of North German, Pommeranian, stock and mainly town dwellers. Most of them were academics, civil servants or teachers, and their lives were mostly spent in various towns of northern Germany. Adelheid's father, Gustav, was also a teacher, and in 1867 he won an appointment in Karlsruhe where, like his counterpart, he became headmaster of a high school. Adelheid's mother was *née* Dohrn, and it is perhaps this branch of the ancestry that shows the strongest signs of musicality. The importance will become clear when we come to speak of Furtwängler's first musical appointment in Breslau.

This is one of the dualities in Furtwängler's character about which we shall have to say more. In heredity he was a mixture of North and South German; he was born in Berlin and, though from the age of eight his home was Munich, he retained the inflection of a Berliner. All his life from 1922 on he felt equally at ease in Berlin and Vienna, though until after the war his home base was always Berlin. On the other hand, from both his parents he inherited a love of humanistic culture, history and the arts which helped to make him what he was.

1. Background

When Adolf and Adelheid first met it was love at first sight. He proposed to her the very first evening they met, but she decided that this was a little too sudden, so they postponed their engagement to the following evening! Although there seem to have been no actual musicians on either side (with the exception of the Dohrns) both families were musical. Adelheid was also a painter of no mean talent.

In Berlin, on 25 January 1886, the first child, a son, was born to Adelheid and Adolf. He was christened in the Lutheran faith, and they gave him the names Gustav Heinrich Ernst Martin *Wilhelm*. Adelheid Furtwängler had a slight facial defect from birth and, as a girl, it gave her something of a complex, especially as her two sisters were, so one reads, real beauties. Her overriding desire was to become the mother of a great and famous son. Little did she know to what an unbelievable extent this wish was to be fulfilled.

In the years to come the Furtwänglers had three more children: a son Walter (1887-1967) and two girls, 'Märit' (1891-1971) (a contraction of Marthe Edith) and Anna (1900-1974), known affectionately as Annele. Throughout their lives these four maintained the best relations, as they did with their mother after their father's early death. They all helped and supported each other, especially Wilhelm, and it is touching to read his letters to them and see how much interest he took in them despite the pressures of his busy life.

Adolf Furtwängler disliked the hectic atmosphere of a big city and always tried to find a residence somewhere on the outskirts to be closer to nature. In Berlin he took a flat near the Nollendorfplatz which overlooked fields and meadows and, when he received his Munich appointment in 1894, the family again lived away from the town in Schwabing. It is hard to believe that a century ago the bustling Nollendorfplatz and Schwabing, now a cross between Soho and Bloomsbury in London terms, should have been 'rural' areas on the outskirts of the city. Things became even better when Adolf Furtwängler acquired a country house, *Haus Tanneck*, on a small peninsula jutting out into the Tegernsee near Bad Wiessee. Here the youngsters could devote themselves to swimming and all sorts of sports and games without being watched by prying neighbours.

3

Furtwängler was a recluse, a 'loner', from his earliest years. The world at large knew him only as an introvert whose whole being and thoughts were concentrated on music and the cultural values of art, literature and philosophy. But throughout his life he remained an ardent sportsman: he loved riding, swimming, tennis, skating and mountaineering; he was also an excellent skier, and mountains always held a bigger attraction for him than flat country or the seaside. He loved walking – and by 'walking' I don't mean just strolling, for on these hikes and expeditions into the mountains he could commune with nature. This is a trait which he must have inherited from his father, and it is this vital union with nature that found its greatest and finest sublimation in his music-making, whether as composer, conductor or pianist. When it came to playing games, it must not be forgotten that Wilhelm was the oldest of the four children. He was also remarkably strong-willed, and he could not bear to lose. Most of the games they played were of his own invention, for he always had to be the leader and he saw to it that the dice were loaded in his favour. If his schemes failed, he simply altered the rules to make sure he won next time.

At his death in 1907 Adolf Furtwängler left *Haus Tanneck* in his will to his four children in equal shares. They continued to use it for holidays. After the war and during the ensuing inflation and depression in Germany, brother Walter, who had studied as an art historian, could not find employment and lived in *Tanneck* with his wife Hilde, who had the brilliant idea of turning it into a Pension to provide a living for the family. Eventually Wilhelm and his sisters gave Walter their shares in the house, and Walter and his family continued to live there. *Haus Tanneck* is now the property of Walter's three surviving sons, two others having been killed in action in the Second World War.

*

At the age of five or six Willi (as he was known to his family and friends) had to begin his schooling in what in England would be called Prep School. Then in Munich (in 1895 or 1896) he started the so-called 'Humanistic Gymnasium', a type of high school where the emphasis was on classics and philosophy. He was a bad pupil. Not that he was inadequate intellectually – in fact, he was always far ahead of his class – but he was bored and disliked authority. He found that his time was better spent on his artistic interests, and in general he regarded school as a waste of time. From an early age he had shown strong artistic leanings. At first it was on the visual side. Though most small children will scrawl on anything given a pencil or a crayon and a surface, be it a piece of paper or a wall, with young Wilhelm it was a more purposeful means of self-expression. And then came music. At about seven, when he had barely learnt to write the alphabet, he asked his mother to explain to him the piano keyboard and the principles of musical notation. She was amazed at the ease with which he absorbed it all. It was as though he already possessed a subconscious knowledge which only had to be awakened; and he took to music as naturally as a duckling to water. On 30 June 1893, when he was about seven and a half, he put on paper his very first composition, *Ein Stückche* (sic) *von den Tieren* ('A Little Piece about Animals'). Adolf Furtwängler, though himself the son of a high school headmaster (or perhaps because of it) had a healthy disdain for the established, organised system of education and its teachers. So, with his great love and understanding of his son, he took the momentous step of taking Wilhelm (then about twelve) away from the treadmill of school routine and of entrusting him to private tutors. Two things may be noted in parenthesis. One is that Wilhelm Furtwängler became the great man he was without benefit of education according to the sacrosanct rules of academic teaching, but purely out of himself, out of his soul, out of his inner being. The other, as an aside, is that Bruno Walter's youth and development proceeded somewhat similarly. It is strange to realise that so many time-honoured conservatoria, music schools and academies have produced many good musicians, but hardly a single genius. Genius is the result of heredity, of environment, of karma. Institutions sometimes help, but more often they hinder.

Willi now had two mentors, both students of his father's: Ludwig Curtius (1874-1954), who acquired fame later as an archaeologist, and Walter Riezler (1878-1965), who was trained as an archaeologist, but became an art historian and a musician. Young Wilhelm was freed from the shackles of scholastic discipline. He could spread his wings, he could absorb knowledge, culture, art to his heart's content, of his own free will and accord; and, with the gifts with which he was endowed by nature, he could blossom forth and become *Furtwängler*. Curtius and Riezler, both splendid men in their own right, exerted a strong influence on Wilhelm from about his thirteenth year. But they were diametrically opposed in their mentality and approach, and Furtwängler profited from both. It may also be mentioned that, from initially being his teachers, both these men formed a firm friendship with him in later years which, despite occasional disagreements, was to last virtually to the end of their days.

It was at the age of seven that little Willi 'decided' to become a composer. It was a decision he never abandoned, for he always regarded composition as his first vocation. His 'Little Piece about Animals' was followed by other compositions, culminating in a setting of Goethe's poem *Die erste Walpurgisnacht*, though he little knew that Mendelssohn had already set the same text to music. All these early compositions are listed under 'Compositions', but it must be stated quite clearly that they are only of theoretical and sentimental value. However, despite all his other interests and those to which his attention was forcibly drawn by Curtius, music remained the overruling passion of his life.

When he was about twelve Furtwängler heard Bach's St Matthew Passion for the first time. It moved him deeply and gave a new perspective to his views on music, both technically and spiritually. Somewhat later came the great impact of Beethoven, whom he placed above all other composers, and it was some time before he realised that Bach and Beethoven were giants of equal stature, neither superior to the other. He was immediately on the defensive if anyone made the slightest detrimental remark about Beethoven, and he had long arguments with Curtius on the Bach-Beethoven issue. Curtius tells in his memoirs of Wilhelm's remarkable assuredness of opinion at a relatively early age and adds, as is confirmed by others, that he always prefaced his arguments with 'As far as I am concerned...' (*Jedenfalls ich ...*).

We get more information about him from Adolf Furtwängler's personal diary entries dating from the winter of 1900/01. '... An astonishing clear vision. Now conscious thinking, analysing, getting to the bottom of formal principles...' We learn that he had started the violin and could already play the second violin part in Haydn quartets, as well as a Mozart violin sonata. When he took his son to Aegina in September 1901, Adolf Furtwängler reports that Wilhelm always had Goethe's poems and letters as well as Beethoven's quartets in his pocket. The latter he studied assiduously, especially the late quartets. Surely an unusual collection of reading matter for a fifteen-year-old on holiday! On Aegina he composed a string sextet, the only youthful composition he ever bothered to mention in later years.

But of course what interests us most is his musical training. As with his general education, he never became a student at any established musical institution and never got any 'letters after his name'. From his mother he received his first piano lessons. Soon after his Aunt Minna, his father's sister and herself a trained piano teacher, took over. His first fully professional tutor was Anton Beer-Walbrunn (1864-1929). Beer-Walbrunn was an organist and composer, but as a composer he never really made his mark and would be forgotten nowadays if he had not also been such a fine Professor of Music. In the first quarter of the twentieth century there were few music students in southern Germany who did not benefit from his teaching. He quickly recognised Wilhelm's extraordinary talents and recommended him to his own teacher, the organist and composer Joseph Rheinberger (1839-1901), at that time Director of the Munich Academy of Music. Rheinberger had ceased to take private pupils, but made an exception in Furtwängler's case. The young rebel gladly submitted to the discipline of this stern taskmaster and was his last and most brilliantly gifted private pupil.

Rheinberger, however, was a reactionary, for whom music finished with Beethoven and the classics and to whom 'revolutionaries' such as Wagner were anathema. But youth longs for progress. Young Wilhelm searched for and found another teacher who could show him the way to Wagner and that form of German romanticism which marks the turn of the century. This was Max von Schillings (1868-1933). Towards the end of his life he said that even if Furtwängler had never achieved those pinnacles of greatness that he later reached he would still have been his 'most interesting student'. Furtwängler later repaid a debt of gratitude by playing von Schillings' works as often as he could. During this period (1902/3) he also returned to Berlin for a short while to study the piano thoroughly with Conrad Ansorge (1862-1930).

It was in 1899 that Ludwig Curtius took charge of young Wilhelm. Two years later he also became the tutor of the son of Adolf von Hildebrand (1847-1921), a well-known sculptor and art historian in Munich with whom the Furtwänglers were well acquainted, and through Curtius this acquaintanceship became firmly established. The Hildebrands had five daughters, all pretty, all intelligent and cultured, and their home was nicknamed *Der Honigtopf* ('The Honey Jar'). Adolf von Hildebrand owned a villa, a former monastery, near Florence, and it was here that the family spent several months each year. Curtius went there in 1902 for the first time with his two 'disciples' and introduced them to all the beauties of Italian, Tuscan, Florentine culture and art. For the young Furtwängler this was an event whose importance cannot be exaggerated: he came face to face with Michelangelo. The experience was overwhelming and, from then on, Beethoven and Michelangelo became irrevocably fused in his mind. Curtius tells of a day when they went together to the Medici Chapel:

> We had decided not to speak in front of the Michelangelo sculptures. Suddenly Willi had vanished and I was getting worried. Finally I found him behind the altar, squatting on the floor, writing music. It was the beginning of his *Te Deum*....

When he was discovered, Wilhelm blushed, for he felt it to be an intrusion into his personal *sanctum*. His inner musical life was always to remain his very own. Years later, after conducting a performance of his Second Symphony, he once said to his wife: 'Whenever I perform a work of my own I feel like a sixteen-year-old girl who has to undress in front of a few old lechers.'

Curtius was instrumental in introducing him to science and to Italian culture, Riezler in laying the foundations of his general appreciation of the visual arts, of *belles-lettres* and, of course, of the philosophical depths of music. His father furthered his interest in Greek culture, especially when he took his son with him in 1901 to his excavations in Aegina. This is one source of Furtwängler's background, and throughout his life classical culture remained the backbone of his attitude to art. Apart from the Greek and Roman classics, he retained his love for great literature, from Shakespeare to Goethe, Kleist and contemporary writers. For some reason Schiller had no appeal for him, but the German philosophers from Kant to Nietzsche were always important.

*

Furtwängler fell violently in love with Bertel von Hildebrand, the youngest and most musical of the five girls, who was one year his junior. It started when they were skating on a lake near Munich, where they went as often as they could – feigning surprise when they met. A little later Wilhelm's mother organised some dancing lessons for the young people of their circle, and Bertel and Wilhelm were happy to see one another there so often. They were engaged in that same winter of 1901/2, but from what one gathers it was not so much a physical as a spiritual love. The letters Furtwängler wrote to his beloved are not emotional effusions, such as most of us may have written at a similar age. True, he expressed his love for Bertel (he once compared her to the Scherzo of Beethoven's Seventh Symphony); but on the whole his letters consisted of discussions of musical and artistic problems which interested him at the time. They are a clear indication of the mental attitude of the young Furtwängler, and he discussed all his problems with her. At the same time shadows of doubt were descending. He did not yet feel himself ready for the bonds of marriage, whereas for her any connection other than marriage was unthinkable. A contributory factor was probably that Bertel had recently become a Roman Catholic. This presumably made her more aware of convention, whereas Wilhelm had all the natural urges of a young man of twenty, was a Lutheran, and had grown up in a spiritual attitude much freer from convention. He voiced his worries to Bertel during a cycling holiday which they took in 1906 from the Brenner Pass via Lake Garda to Florence in company of Bertel's sister and her fiancé, and broached the matter again in a letter. The engagement was dissolved some months later. Eventually she married the composer Walter Braunfels, and Furtwängler suffered agonies and torment for some time to come. There can be no doubt that she was one of the few deep loves of his life.

In the appendix to Furtwängler's letters (p.289), Frank Thiess writes about this love between Wilhelm and Bertel. I cannot do better than quote him:

> The story of his youthful love gives the most important insight into Furtwängler's development from boy to youth and from youth to man. By comparison, the question whether the feelings which his betrothed had towards him corresponded to his own love is of little importance, for what Bertel von Hildebrand meant to him is more important than the fact that she was incapable of giving him that for which he yearned. During the six decisive years of his maturing she brought him a rare understanding, she prevented him from entering into light-hearted relationships, and she accompanied him lovingly in his own spiritual atmosphere of highest endeavour. In this way she furthered his inner development to the greatest possible extent, always considering his stormy and restless character. Especially she recognised what lofty thoughts were striving to be realised in this highly gifted young man, and thereby she helped him to know himself. She saw his talents clearly and also understood the nobility of his soul as a priceless gift. In this way she took away from him all his self-discontent, all the nagging doubts as regards the necessity of his character, which he himself could not overcome.

Furtwängler was ready for the world. The foundations had been laid, and he was set on being a composer. The thought of becoming a conductor had not yet entered his mind.

2

The Beginnings: 1905–1911

The year 1905 must be regarded as an essential turning point in Furtwängler's life. He was now 19 and clear in his mind about how he wished to shape his future. On the other hand he realised how much he still had to learn, for he always wanted to go into everything thoroughly and to be completely knowledgeable on all fronts. He felt he needed experience in practical matters – of which he was then quite ignorant – connected with opera and concert life in general. With the assistance of the conductor Georg Dohrn, a cousin on his mother's side who was in charge of the musical life of Breslau, he took a job as repetiteur at the Municipal Theatre of that town for the season 1905/6.

It was not a particularly brilliant position. He had to rehearse with the chorus and the singers, and the only conducting he was allowed to do was directing the off-stage music in a few of the operas. But although he was on the bottom rung he made an impression on everyone he came in contact with. First there was his incredible ability to sight-read easily and accurately even the most difficult piano reductions of opera scores. Then there was the way he played the piano: he played not just with his hands, but with his legs, his face, his whole head and body, throwing himself into the music like one possessed. In Breslau he was known as 'that blonde, good-looking, tall young man', for he could still boast a head of fair curly hair. Few of us who knew him can remember him like that! Moreover the height, which has often been emphasised, is greatly exaggerated. In fact he was 5 ft 11 ins tall. The impression of height he gave was due to his slim figure – and his radiating personality.

The constant contact with the professional world, with singers and orchestral musicians, was of paramount importance to his development. It was a rude awakening for a young man who had lived hitherto in a rarefied atmosphere of musical ideals to find that when it came to practical experience and everyday necessities ideals sometimes had to be sacrificed. This was not in his character at all. Compromise was always anathema to him. But though he was only occasionally able to conduct, he soon realised that he had an innate aptitude for it. Perhaps already then he 'tasted blood'. This constant struggle between the two souls, that of the composer and that of the conductor, dwelt within him till the day of his death.

It was in Breslau that his first orchestral composition, an early Symphony in D, received its first performance under the baton of Georg Dohrn.[1] To say that it did not go down well would be an understatement: it was utterly condemned by both the audience and the critics. Father and son were deeply affected by the débâcle but were not daunted. They both determined that they had to make good the defeat, and Wilhelm decided that the best way to vindicate himself would be to conduct a concert in Munich, with a programme which would include another composition.

Though he was at the top of his profession, Adolf Furtwängler was not a rich man: academics were no better paid in those days than they are now, and hiring a full symphony orchestra and a hall, not to mention all the expenses involved in mounting a concert, were clearly beyond his means. What he did have were contacts in the intellectual and artistic world of Munich, among them Franz Kaim who had formed his own orchestra. Adolf asked Kaim to give his son a date and, as the renown of that 'incredibly gifted young Furtwängler' had already spread through Munich musical circles, the request was quickly granted. Furtwängler decided on his own programme: Beethoven's Overture 'The Consecration of the House', an Adagio in B minor of his own and, for the second half, Bruckner's Symphony No.9! Furtwängler never made things easy for himself, and with the Bruckner Symphony he had chosen what

[1] This work must not be confused with the official Symphony No.1 in B minor which, in the main, was composed in 1938-41 and completed shortly after the end of the Second World War.

is conceivably one of the greatest, most difficult and most problematical works in the established classical repertoire. This from a young man who had never yet conducted a symphony orchestra! The orchestra was aghast. When this youth of twenty came to the first rehearsal and stood before them, conducting in a completely uncontrolled manner, throwing himself around with arms flailing, walking about on the rostrum, never keeping still for a moment, there was a feeling of consternation and a belief that the concert would never take place. But, lo and behold, the inexperienced youth soon proved his mettle. He quickly demonstrated that he knew precisely what he wanted: that, despite the deficiencies of his conducting technique, he was aware of the tone colour of every instrument and of how these colours should be blended. The concert took place and, although Furtwängler himself later remarked that he had 'somehow managed to scrape through the Bruckner' (*Ich habe mich schlecht und recht durchgeschlagen*), the orchestra was satisfied. They were aware, even then, of his magnetic personality and authority. The audience was overwhelmed by the passion with which he made music, and even the critics condescended to give him paternal words of encouragement, if not praise. So we may safely regard that concert in June 1906 as the birth of Wilhelm Furtwängler the Conductor.

Though he in no way deviated from his ambition to become a composer, Furtwängler was now old enough to realise that it would be almost impossible to earn a living at it. In those days in Central Europe it was always possible, given the talents he possessed, to survive as a conductor at one of the many opera houses. But the thought of making this his life work was repugnant, as he wrote to Bertel during that winter 1905/6:

> Ever to become a theatre conductor seems more impossible to me than ever... You simply don't know how much bad music there is, you can't imagine it, ...and people...find it all beautiful and lovely and wallow around in it like pigs in the mud. All great music like Mozart, Beethoven seems so direct, so unostentatious by comparison. It is inevitable that such audiences find it boring.

Nevertheless there was the economic necessity. In his diary entries Adolf Furtwängler once voiced a suspicion that his son's move in that direction might be prompted partly by Bertel's urging him into marriage. 'Girls always want to get married,' he noted, 'and young men must first get to know life and achieve something.'

Wilhelm applied for, and obtained, a post as repetiteur and assistant conductor at the Zürich Municipal Theatre for the 1906/7 season. The director was kindly disposed towards him and permitted him occasionally to conduct an operetta. At that time *The Merry Widow* was the hit of the season, and Furtwängler was allowed to conduct it. In later years he said with a smile that he conducted it for the first time as though it had been *Götterdämmerung*, but this initial enthusiasm soon waned. By the third performance he was completely and utterly bored, and when he had to do it for the ninth time, in one of these sections of spoken dialogues which form an intrinsic part of any operetta, he happily drifted off into cloud-cuckoo-land and his own dream-world. Unconsciously it appeared to him that this scene had lasted rather longer than usual. Little realising that the actors had said their cue lines more than once, he failed to come in with the orchestra. The third time round the tenor strode to the ramp and said, in effect, 'Well, if you don't want to...' (*Na, dann eben nicht!*) and stalked off the stage in a fury. The sequel was unavoidable. There are two versions of the story. One is that the director called for him and said with a grin, 'I don't think you ever will become a conductor of operettas', and relieved him of his duties for the rest of the season. The other, less probable but more picturesque, is that he told his staff manager: 'Give that young man the sack – he'll never become a conductor anyway!' Whatever the truth, that was the inglorious end of Furtwängler's second professional appointment.

The next important stages were two years in Munich and two in Strasbourg. But before we come to these we must mention another event which cast a shadow over his life. On 10 October 1907 his father died, aged 54. He had returned to Greece, already ill, to take up his researches and excavations in Aegina. His illness was not considered serious, but was fatal. Adolf Furtwängler, whose spiritual home was Greece, was no doubt glad to die in surroundings which he loved and which were his life, and he was buried with public honours in the Protestant Cemetery of Athens. A marble replica of the Sphinx which he had himself excavated was placed above his tomb. But for Wilhelm the loss of his father, with whom he had been extremely close, was a great shock, though needless to say, introvert that he was, we find next to nothing in his letters and diary notes concerning his personal emotions.

For the two seasons 1907/9 he worked as repetiteur at the Court Opera in Munich, where Felix Mottl was his 'Chief'. There would have been no better tutor than Mottl for a promising young musician, for what Mottl did not know about opera and music in general was not worth knowing. Furtwängler profited to the full from this experience, and was eventually engaged as third conductor at the Opera of Strasbourg, where Hans Pfitzner had recently taken over as musical director. Furtwängler was seventeen years Pfitzner's junior, and it was indeed a privilege to study and absorb the knowledge of so great a master of conducting and neo-romantic composition. Pfitzner recognised the talents of his young sub-conductor and helped him in every possible way. Furtwängler was soon allowed to conduct Maillart's *Les Dragons de Villars* (known in German as *Das Glöckchen des Eremiten*), as well as run-of-the-mill operas such as *Martha* and *L'Elisire d'amore*. He was not particularly taken by this trite repertoire, but it enabled him to acquire the foundations of a conducting technique. Moreover, co-operating with a man of Pfitzner's calibre on great operas such as *Der Freischütz, Fidelio* and *Tannhäuser* gave him profound insight and a basis for his future work.

Furtwängler realised his shortcomings only too well and was desperately anxious to improve his conducting technique, so as to reconcile the actual sounds of orchestra and ensemble with his own musical imagination. Strangely, two apparently irrelevant matters were of help. One was that he was basically uninterested in social life and happiest on his own. The other was his chronic insomnia, from which he had suffered since his teens, especially when some new composition was burgeoning in his mind. So, after a performance, he would not retire to bed, but, no matter how bad the weather, would sally forth into the dark streets of Strasbourg, humming to himself – and conducting whole operas. On these nocturnal walks, or at home alone in his room, he would rethink all those passages that had

15

not worked out to his satisfaction in the performance, searching with his baton for new ways of expression. (This habit of conducting to himself remained with him for the rest of his life and has led to the idiotic story that he was a *poseur* who rehearsed his movements in front of a mirror so that he could make an impression on his audience.) An unfortunate side-effect was that when he next came to conduct the same opera he tried to put his new findings into practice, which must have been bewildering for orchestra and singers alike.

Furtwängler was regarded very favourably by his Strasbourg audiences, but the reviews were either lukewarm or negative. Rudolf Louis, one of the leading critics of southern Germany, said that he was 'completely hopeless: he would never become a conductor worth his salt.' More important perhaps was his contact with the Pfitzners. Hans Pfitzner became almost a father figure, and Pfitzner's wife kept a motherly eye on him: in later years he unburdened himself of his personal worries in his letters to her. As with Max von Schillings, Furtwängler retained his affection for Pfitzner and gave many performances of his works in later years.

We must now take a look at his compositions during this period. After the fiasco of his early symphony in Breslau he settled down to write a second symphony, but he only completed one movement, *Largo*. It is this movement, in a revised form, that he performed in his first symphony concert in Munich in 1906 under the title *Symphonic Adagio*. Many years later it was partly the basis of the opening movement of the official Symphony No.1. In 1906 in Zürich he began writing his *Te Deum* for which he had made the first sketches in the Medici Chapel in Florence in 1902. He completed it in 1909. In my opinion it can be regarded as the first of his fully valid compositions, though it still betrays a certain awkwardness. It had its first performance in Breslau in 1910, again under the direction of Georg Dohrn. Again it was slated by the critics, but at least this time it was received more favourably by the public. Furtwängler was invited to conduct a performance of it in Strasbourg in 1911, and it was subsequently performed in Essen in 1914 under Hermann Abendroth, whom Furtwängler succeeded in Lübeck, and in Leipzig in 1915 under the great *Thomaskantor* Karl Straube.

16

2. The Beginnings: 1905–1911

After the completion of the *Te Deum*, and as his phenomenal rise as a conductor took up more of his time, little scope for composition remained to him. Being a meticulous and conscientious worker, he was never satisfied, but always intent on revising, improving, perfecting. It is not surprising that he did not appear before the public as a composer for a quarter of a century.

Furtwängler's two seasons in Strasbourg came to an end in the spring of 1911. He was appointed conductor of the orchestra in Lübeck, where he took up his duties in September, another great milestone in his life.

3

Lübeck and Mannheim: 1911–1922

In 1911 Hermann Abendroth (1883-1956) resigned as conductor of the Lübeck orchestra, a post he had held since 1905, to take up a similar position in Essen. Ida Boy-Ed (1852-1928), a well-known writer of those days, who was a personal friend of Furtwängler's mother, suggested that her son should apply for the position. Actually it was too late: there had been almost a hundred applicants of whom four had been short-listed. Moreover, it had already been decided privately that one Rudolf Siegel was to get the job. The secret leaked out, however, and one of the four candidates retracted his application. Lübeck was in a dilemma, for it was the usual custom to have four 'finalists' who had to be chosen out of the original applicants. The young Furtwängler, however, represented no danger to their favourite as he was still unknown and had not yet made his mark as an orchestral conductor. He was therefore allowed to become one of the four from whom the final choice had to be made.

Furtwängler was invited to conduct a trial rehearsal and concert in April 1911. As the Musical Director in Lübeck was in charge not only of the symphony concerts but also of the Philharmonic Choir, the first test consisted of a choir rehearsal, with the members of the municipal jury seated at the back of the choir, watching with eagle eye. This disconcerted Furtwängler, and he confessed to Frau Boy-Ed afterwards that he had made a mess of it. However, at the orchestral rehearsal next day the jury sat behind him in the hall, and after a minute or two he forgot all about them, absorbed in the music. Although his style of conducting was completely different from that of the austere, well-controlled Abendroth, the orchestra went with him. With a sixth sense musicians know a musician when they meet one, and during the rehearsal some members said to him: 'We of the orchestra want you and nobody else!' Once again the magic of Furtwängler's personality, the miracle of his magnetism, even at this early age, had won him a victory over professionalism and routine.

Furtwängler was unanimously appointed Abendroth's successor. It is perhaps amusing to remember in passing that, years later, Abendroth was to be one of *his* successors as conductor of the *Gewandhaus* Orchestra in Leipzig. In a town like Lübeck news travels fast, and what the orchestra says one day the 'upper class' says the next. Furtwängler became the talk of the town.

It is perhaps necessary to say a few words about Lübeck. In the thirteenth century it was the headquarters of the famous Hanseatic League and for a century and a half it retained its commercial predominance in northern Europe. Gradually its importance waned, and now, with Hamburg and Bremen, it is only one of the three surviving 'Free Hanseatic Towns'. But two features of these towns remain. First, as they are ports lying on or near the sea, they possess a spirit of open-mindedness towards the wide world. Secondly, they are self-willed, and dominated in their municipal government by patrician families. These families not only govern the town but direct its culture. They represent the élite, and are proud of it. Thomas Mann, who was born in Lübeck, came from such a family, and he gave immortality to that way of life in his famous novel *Buddenbrooks*. Another of these patrician families was the Dieckmanns. Most of them were musically inclined, and many had regular music-making in their houses. Furtwängler, who was always averse to social life, was welcomed with open arms, particularly by Frau Lilli Dieckmann. We are fortunate that she corresponded regularly with her mother, and from these letters we gain insight into Furtwängler's days in Lübeck.

On receiving his Lübeck appointment Furtwängler was beset as usual by doubts and indecisions. Was he ready for the job? Was he worthy of it? He was on the point of turning it down, and it took all Frau Boy-Ed's powers of persuasion to make him accept: in later years he was to be very grateful to her. In Lübeck his duties were exclusively those of an orchestral conductor. He had to conduct the eight big symphony concerts of the season, at least two choral concerts with the Philharmonic Choir, and also the popular concerts on Wednesdays. These consisted of three parts. The first was classical music (though on the light side), the second was mainly solo performances, and the third was plain rumbustious. They may be compared to Henry Wood's Promenade Concerts. Like Wood, Abendroth had tried to steer them into more serious channels. Furtwängler followed in his footsteps. By the time he had left Lübeck and conducted his last popular concert, on 28 April 1915, he could present his audience with a programme of Bach, Beethoven, Weber, Brahms, Liszt and Wagner. All *schmaltzy* items had been eliminated. Nevertheless he later admitted that in these popular concerts he gained experience in conducting, because he could experiment.

The official symphony concerts were a different matter. Here he really had to be on the alert. He had never been one to listen to the acknowledged conductors of his day and form his opinion on the strength of their performances: he could read a score and make up his own mind from the image it produced in him through his inner ear. To give but one example: in Lübeck he conducted the Fifth Symphony of Tchaikovsky for the first time without ever having heard it before and, after the rehearsal, rang Frau Dieckmann to ask: 'Was it all right? Were the tempi all right? I was not well enough prepared: one should know the score by heart, otherwise one just stumbles around blindfold.' During his years in Lübeck he also conducted for the first time Beethoven's Ninth. Naturally we have no recording of it, but from the reports of others it must have been overwhelming. Those who heard it say that they had never heard such a Ninth before and never expect to again.

Although it was outside his duties, Furtwängler soon achieved such a reputation that the Director of the Lübeck Opera invited him as a guest. He conducted *Fidelio*, *The Merry Wives of Windsor* and *Meistersinger*. So, in a way, Lübeck meant for him the fusion of his gifts as a symphony conductor with his gifts as an opera conductor which he had already brought with him from Strasbourg.

3. Lübeck and Mannheim: 1911–1922

To trace Furtwängler's life during these four years in Lübeck it is best to go back to Frau Dieckmann's letters to her mother that we have already mentioned. They not only give details about the musician, but also provide charming glimpses of his private life.

Though it was not till the autumn of 1911 that he started officially – he conducted his first symphony concert of the 1911/12 season in October – his name was on everybody's lips from the day he conducted his 'trial concert' in April. Frau Dieckmann wrote:

> Whenever you meet acquaintances, you don't ask about their state of health or the 'dear little ones' – already from a distance of some metres you call to each other: 'How marvellous, Furtwängler!' – these three words say everything.

In September he moved to Lübeck, which was to remain his home until spring 1915. Unlike his predecessor he was in no way a man of fashion, and he was happiest when he could go for long rambles in the countryside. But there were occasions when certain conventions had to be observed, especially during the first weeks of September when he was obliged to make a number of courtesy calls. Frau Dieckmann once saw him leaving his house wearing an enormous top hat which, she presumed, had been forced on him by Frau Boy-Ed. Judging by this account, it must have been a funny sight. But there is also a letter dated September 1911, from which I shall quote at length, as it shows up both the musician and the rather awkward grown-up boy he still was.

> About last night I must tell you that we had the tall, slim, yet athletic Furtwängler...as our guest... What an extraordinary personality! Edgy and angular, outspoken to the point of brusqueness, clumsy as a child. ...But when he starts to talk one feels at once the nobility of his spirit and the universality of his cultural background, and when he sits down at the piano the whole of his great artistic soul opens up – a soul of the most refined tenderness without any striving for effect – a pondering, a searching, a finding and loosing oneself – giving his entire being to the world of music.
>
> He played Beethoven's [Sonata] op.109, and the impression was nothing less than shattering. It was as if he himself was creating it on the spur of the moment, like a key to his soul. And at the end, he was so furious and would have liked to have thrown my Bechstein at me. Thank

God he wasn't strong enough to do so and only threw many rude words at me such as that it was disgusting 'to have such a chopping-block stand in such an ideal music room'....

He wore a pair of horrible boots with which, presumably, he had recently been hiking across the moors and at which he himself looked aghast with amazement.... We teased our big lad mercilessly about those boots, and he asked me quite seriously 'whether he would have to buy patent leather shoes for the symphony concert' – for him obviously the quintessence of a dandy!

Patent leather shoes or no, Furtwängler at that time certainly had not yet learned 'stage deportment'. During the applause at the end of a concert he would stand with his back to the audience and bring an enormous handkerchief out of his trouser pocket. Then he would wipe the sweat from his face, his neck and even his hair. Only after this ceremonial had been performed would he turn, take his bow and acknowledge the acclaim.

Frau Dieckmann was present at the final rehearsal for his first symphony concert in October 1911. Already in these early days (he was then only 25) he showed his 'powers of suggestion to which both orchestra and audience succumb'. She adds:

The outward manners of Furtwängler, it must be admitted, are still indescribably funny. He waves his arms like a windmill and contorts his face in the most ghastly grimaces. The legs have specific motions of their own, so that the whole appears a tumult without parallel. But all this one forgives and forgets when the music reaches one's ears....

A couple of months later, when she had attended one of the popular concerts with Frau Boy-Ed:

We were delighted both by Furtwängler's talents and by his movements. At one point, in the heat of the moment, he even stuck out his tongue a good ten centimetres.

But then he conducted the Prelude to *Tristan* with such maturity and yearning, so movingly and sorrowfully, that one would not have noticed his tongue even if he had used it to beat time....

Furtwängler was only too aware of the deficiencies of his conducting technique, and he continued the method of training of his Strasbourg days. He would roam the streets of Lübeck at night in his shapeless raincoat and equally shapeless hat, humming and grunting to himself while gesticulating and conducting wildly. One night there was an amusing incident. A policeman took him for a drunk and promptly marched him off to the police station. However, the error was quickly cleared up and Furtwängler was allowed to go home. Yet this method of training soon bore fruit, and by February 1912 Frau Dieckmann could report to her mother:

> Furtwängler gains in stature from one concert to the next and keeps us all enthralled. His movements, too, are becoming more disciplined and more eloquent. His left hand cannot be described – it entices or calms [the players] with a gentle vibrating of his fingertips, as if a butterfly quivers with its wings....

It has been noted that Furtwängler rarely attended concerts given by other conductors. He once told Frau Dieckmann that 'he didn't think much of Schuch and Weingartner. The latter was too extrovert for him, and he found that he could not learn from either of them.' But he did go to a concert in Hamburg under Nikisch[1] in February 1912 in the company of Frau Dieckmann. During the train journey he told her that he would come into the artists' room after the concert – would Frau Dieckmann introduce him to Nikisch? Considering his disparaging remarks about Schuch and Weingartner, she was rather apprehensive and said he must say a few words of praise – to which he replied: 'I shall only do that if I like the concert.' To continue in her words:

> The concert was ravishing and, to my great delight, I saw Furtwängler applauding with absolute enthusiasm. Then he came down to the artists' room and Nikisch, whose attention I had already drawn to our young genius in August, gave him both his hands and expressed his joy at meeting him, the 'oft-mentioned young friend of my friend'. During the whole scene Furtwängler failed to get out a single word, although he was truly enthusiastic, and only smiled down with some embarrassment at the much smaller Nikisch. But when Nikisch, in his heart-felt way, invited him to supper with us or – he added as a little joke – 'Perhaps a young gentleman finds it more interesting to stroll about the big town by himself', Furtwängler only uttered a terse 'That is so!' – and that ended the conversation.

*

[1] Arthur Nikisch (1855-1922) was the greatest conductor in Germany, if not in the world, in those days. He was the Chief Conductor of both the *Gewandhaus* Orchestra in Leipzig (since 1895) and of the Berlin Philharmonic (since 1897). He retained both these positions until his death.

A few hours later, when it was time to catch the train back to Lübeck, Frau Dieckmann found Furtwängler already sitting in the compartment, disgruntled, disgusted with himself and furious at his own behaviour. He said that he had let slip the apparently rude words only because he had thought that Nikisch's kind invitation had been a courteous platitude, and that he was considered an unavoidable appendage to herself. Nevertheless Nikisch was, and remained, the only conductor whom Furtwängler really respected and from whom he could learn. He became a regular guest at Nikisch's suppers after concerts, though even then, with his over-sensitive nature, he still considered himself neglected. He felt that rather than just address the odd question to him Nikisch should converse with him for an hour or so, 'and then he would know who I am'.

It fascinated Furtwängler to try to discover Nikisch's secret, why music sounded so perfect, so different, under his baton. It could be said that Nikisch was his only teacher. Furtwängler was one of the few who did not decry Nikisch as a showman. He once explained to Frau Dieckmann how each of Nikisch's sparing movements was designed only to have an effect on the orchestra, to be translated into music. Years later he told someone, 'If ever I get to Berlin, there can be no doubt that I shall become Nikisch's successor', little knowing that the person he was talking to was Werner Wolff, the son of Louise Wolff, who was the queen of Berlin's musical life, much as Emmie Tillett was the queen of London's. It is interesting to cite a view from the other side. Carl Hagemann (with whom Furtwängler was to work so closely in his Mannheim years, when Hagemann was the *Intendant* of the Mannheim Opera) describes an occasion in Hamburg where Furtwängler was often a guest at the suppers given by Nikisch:

Occasionally a very tall and very pale young man, always dressed rather sloppily, used to turn up at these gatherings. They told me that he was the conductor of the Municipal Orchestra in Lübeck and had come over for the concert. In those days he struck me particularly by his appetite and his taciturnity, but when he did say something, it was always to the point. One day Nikisch took me aside and, in his kindly way, pointed out this young man who was sitting there so unobtrusively. He added that he was surely destined for great things and, if he was not deceived, would probably become his successor.

3. Lübeck and Mannheim: 1911–1922

Incidentally, when Furtwängler went from Lübeck to Hamburg – in those days of course by train – he always travelled third class. This was observed by a member of the orchestral committee, who chided him gently saying that the Principal Conductor of the town of Lübeck really should travel second class. This took him aback, for he well remembered that his own father – who was, after all, a person of eminence – had never travelled anything but third class on the railways!

On the lighter side there is an amusing episode which also falls into the early part of 1912. Frau Dieckmann always referred to 'our circle', a group of about six who were happy and relaxed in each other's company and of whom, of course, Furtwängler was one. A date had been set for a kind of private ball at a friend's house, and before the event Frau Dieckmann had arranged to give Furtwängler some dancing lessons which, in themselves, must have been hilarious enough. Furtwängler, not unusually, arrived some 45 minutes late and was very contrite. Frau Dieckmann, paraphrasing the *Marschallin* in *Rosenkavalier*, writes: 'And then I still had to console the lad.' They went to the party. As the place was crowded, they retreated to an attic with their little group and made themselves as comfortable as they could. Discovering a basket of unironed washing they began dressing themselves up as though for a fancy dress ball. Furtwängler danced so wildly that, with his shirt flying up, it was 'positively dangerous'.

Furtwängler, even in those days, was no speechifier. When he came to conduct the last choir rehearsal of the 1911/12 season he found his desk garlanded with flowers, topped with a beautiful bunch of roses. He shoved the roses under the desk and conducted the rehearsal. At the end, of course, the choir expected a few words from him and waited with bated breath. All they got was the memorable statement: 'In any case, the pleasure was entirely yours.' On another occasion he managed to get out a couple of sentences. While he was searching for the next words, his eyes dropped to the score and the speech was forgotten. He just raised his baton and said: 'Letter F, please!'

With the beginning of the First World War nobody knew what the future would hold. Fortunately Furtwängler was not called up. But he did not seem happy about that, thinking it might be quite fun to 'guard a bridge'. Frau Dieckmann commented: 'He probably thought that it might be very nice to do some fishing!'

In March 1914 he conducted Bruckner's Symphony No.8. Frau Dieckmann writes:

> After the one and half hours of the performance we were all as in a dream, and we didn't want to wake up out of this deep reverie. In the *Adagio* there was hardly one of us who had a dry eye. Later Szanto [the leader of the orchestra] told us that at times he had hardly been able to read the music because his eyes were overflowing with tears.

Similarly in January 1915:

> Our whole being is still elevated by the incomparable, lofty experience of last night. Furtwängler – *Eroica!* – I came to know it under Schuch – Weingartner disclosed it to me – Nikisch enthused me – but Furtwängler shook us to the bones: he is a Titan, who recreated this work anew.

She also reports enthusiastically about his performances of *Meistersinger* and *Fidelio*.

*

In 1914 Arthur Bodansky (1877-1939) decided to leave Mannheim to accept an offer in the USA. Mannheim was one of the leading centres in Germany. We must remember that Germany was once split up politically into 350 or more principalities, until, in 1871 under Bismarck, it was welded back into national unity. Every little prince, duke, king or potentate had his domain, and each one wanted his Court Theatre, Court Orchestra, Court Opera. This was of great benefit to German culture, though a disadvantage to Germany's economic and political standing. Mannheim was one of these places, presided over by *Kurfürst* Karl Theodor. Already in the eighteenth century it had exerted its influence on none other than Wolfgang Amadeus Mozart by its tradition of the 'Mannheim School', with the Mannheim style of orchestral playing and composition, whose father was Johann Stamitz. This great tradition has been handed down to the present day, and Furtwängler was to become one of the links in the chain.

Mannheim was anxious to have a really big name as its chief conductor and would have liked to see Nikisch in the position, but it set its sights too high. Two factors that led eventually to Furtwängler's appointment were particularly important, however incongruous. The first was a recommendation from Bruno Walter (Furtwängler's senior by ten years), who was then *Generalmusikdirektor* in Munich. He described Furtwängler as 'one of the most inspired of the up-and-coming young conductors, even though still lacking experience in the operatic field'. The other was more prosaic: the Musical Director of the Lübeck Opera had also applied for the post, and a jury of five representatives from the Mannheim theatre, headed by Bodansky, had therefore to come to Lübeck anyway. First they heard the other candidate, who conducted Smetana's *Bartered Bride*. According to Furtwängler himself, it was a brilliant performance. Furtwängler was quite certain that he was out of the running. After all, apart from the famous Zürich *Merry Widow* and the few light operas he had conducted in Strasbourg, his repertoire was limited to the three operas he had been invited to conduct in Lübeck. The next evening it was his turn: *Fidelio*. He had done his utmost during rehearsals but, according to those who heard him, the rehearsals had been pretty disastrous. At one point the leading tenor, who had to sing the vital part of the First Prisoner, told him that 'it was just as a personal favour that he had condescended to take on such a trivial role'. Furtwängler went mad and yelled at him: 'You miserable so-and-so, shut your dirty trap!' Then, rushing through the orchestra on to the stage, he tried to get at him. If the rest of the cast and the chorus had not restrained him, Lübeck would have been the poorer by one tenor. With all this preceding excitement the chorus was at its worst on the night, even though, from what one reads, there must have been moments of magic beauty.

When the opera was over Furtwängler changed. He was about to go home in the deepest dejection when he was suddenly informed that the members of the Mannheim committee were expecting him in the *Ratskeller*. He went along with a shrug expecting them to say kindly: 'Awfully sorry, but...'. To his surprise they received him with the utmost courtesy and began to discuss the performance with him. A man of Bodansky's calibre and experience had obviously noticed everything that had gone wrong, but he added: 'You have done wonders with the orchestra.' When it came to the choir Furtwängler admitted in despair that it had been absolutely terrible. Then Bodansky said: 'I know, but then, in Mannheim you will have a much better choir at your disposal.' Furtwängler was speechless as the realisation of what was implied sank in. Later he described it as the greatest joy of his life.

It may have been the best moment for Furtwängler and a great step in his career, but for Lübeck it was the parting knell. The news was soon common knowledge throughout the town, and in March 1915 Frau Dieckmann wrote to her mother: 'Now the blow has struck – Furtwängler leaves us for Mannheim.' Of the last symphony concert he conducted in Lübeck, in April, she writes: 'It was heavenly – but *so* sad. Most people had tears in their eyes, and Frau Boy-Ed was inconsolable.' Roses and laurels were showered upon him, and the leader of the orchestra was deathly pale as he handed him a wreath on their behalf. His last official appearance as a conductor took place in the same month when he conducted a popular concert. He was deeply moved, and his parting speech consisted of just a few words, spoken in the soft voice of a child battling against incipient tears. 'I just want to tell you that I am deeply grateful for your friendship and sympathy. I shall never forget Lübeck.'

In a letter of April 1915 Frau Dieckmann writes to her mother of these last days in Lübeck:

> One afternoon Furtwängler came to see me once more all by himself. His Mannheim position is marvellous – he is like a king and can take all decisions. He himself has declared from the start that he would only conduct two operas by Mozart, one by Gluck, *Fidelio*, *Meistersinger*, the *Ring* and *Parsifal*.
>
> In our minds we allowed all the richness of the past four years to pass before us, from the merriest moments to the most holy.... Oh yes, even those popular concerts we remembered, when his dog Lord would appear quite unconcernedly during the music, cross the auditorium, and make a straight line for his beloved Master.

Shortly before he was due to leave, Frau Dieckmann gave a little supper party for the intimate circle of their friends, instructing everybody to come in evening dress in his honour. He himself arrived three-quarters of an hour late, in dust-covered shoes and a casual grey suit. As she put it: 'He remained true to his own self up to the last.'

*

Furtwängler took up his new appointment as *Hofkapellmeister* ('Court Conductor') in Mannheim in September 1915. The situation was completely novel to him. Breslau, Zürich, Munich and Strasbourg had been apprentice years: he had been involved in opera but had done almost no conducting. In Lübeck he had been basically a symphony conductor, though he had also conducted three operas. Now, all of a sudden, he found himself the director of an opera – the only time in his life incidentally that he ever held such a position exclusively – without either knowing the routine or having managerial experience. That he also had to conduct six or so symphony concerts, the so-called 'Academies', was almost a secondary matter.

In the Hanseatic town of Lübeck, as we have noted, municipal and social life was governed by the patrician families; but Mannheim, like Berlin, Frankfurt and many other towns, was ruled by well-to-do families who had acquired their standing as lawyers, merchants and bankers. In Germany, as in most European countries, there had been an undertow of anti-semitism – this was no invention of the Nazis, though they carried the tendency to unprecedented lengths. In the course of time Jews had been prevented from entering certain professions and careers and, being deprived of these privileges, had had to turn to financial and business enterprises. From these 'underdogs' stemmed the great mercantile and banking families in Europe. These wealthy families were at the root of German culture and philosophy. Their ancestry went back to the Middle Ages; they felt themselves to be entirely German. The question of creed was an individual matter, and indeed many Jews had converted to Christianity. Their Mosaic origin was only discovered when, after 1933, Hitler issued the so-called 'Nuremberg Laws'. These were at the same time criminal, idiotic and destructive of the best of Germany's cultural heritage.

In one way, however, things were much the same in Mannheim as in Lübeck. Both Furtwängler's predecessors,

Hermann Abendroth and Arthur Bodansky, had been 'society lions', precisely the opposite of Furtwängler. Furtwängler was happiest when he was on his own or in the company of his dog Lord. In a conversation later with Riess he described himself as 'a badger who likes to crawl into his sett'. The people of Mannheim, like the people of Lübeck, soon fell in love with 'their' Furtwängler and came to understand that a man who conducted so much, who gave so much of himself, who had so many scores to study, could not be bothered with official receptions. On the other hand he found many friends who gladly opened their doors to him, where he could be at home in a small circle, and where there was music-making among friends and amateurs as well as stimulating conversation on the sort of cultural level he had been accustomed to from his earliest days. One such family was the Geissmars. The head of the family, Dr Geissmar himself, was a prominent lawyer of Jewish descent whose ruling passion was music. He himself was an excellent amateur violinist who spared no money when it came to buying a new violin. He had a Stradivarius. Many famous musicians were guests in the Geissmar home, and he himself was such an enthusiast that he even kept a violin in his office, so that he could play a few notes whenever he had a spare moment. Furtwängler needed no introduction, as there was a family connection dating back to the days of his grandmother. Indeed a string quartet he had written at about fifteen had its 'première' at the home of the Geissmars. Needless to say, he was a frequent guest in the house.

This close personal relationship had one far-reaching consequence. The Geissmars had a daughter, Berta (1892-1949). Nobody claims that she was a beauty, but in such a household it was inevitable that she should have imbibed music from babyhood onwards, and she was a not inconsiderable string player. She was also highly intelligent. Furtwängler became very fond of her and they often discussed art and philosophy. It should perhaps be stressed (in view of later rumours) that there was never anything between them except friendship, understanding and mutual respect. Berta Geissmar studied in Heidelberg and eventually received a doctorate in philosophy from Frankfurt University, but she was always somewhat shy in the presence of Furtwängler.

3. Lübeck and Mannheim: 1911–1922

It is charming to read in her memoirs (p.18) of the occasion on which they became real friends. They had met by accident at a reception given to some Heidelberg professor (Furtwängler moved freely in university circles) and had afterwards made their way home together. Berta Geissmar writes:

> It was early summer, and when we came to the ancient bridge over the Neckar, facing the castle ruin, there sat a little shrivelled old woman selling the first cherries. Furtwängler bought a bagful, and said: 'Now let's see who can spit the stones the furthest.' So we stood spitting our stones into the Neckar; it was great fun, and this playful moment sealed our lifelong friendship.

When Furtwängler resigned from his post in Mannheim at the end of the 1919/20 season and moved to Berlin, he suggested that Berta too should come to Berlin. She agreed and moved there in autumn 1921. For the next fourteen years, until she was compelled to leave Germany and settled in England, she remained Furtwängler's secretary. Eventually she took over much of the day-to-day management of the Berlin Philharmonic, especially the organising of their national and international tours. It is interesting to note that her collaboration with Furtwängler and the Berlin Philharmonic (1921-35) lasted almost as long as her later collaboration with Sir Thomas Beecham and the London Philharmonic (1936-1949).

*

Concerning the five seasons Furtwängler spent in Mannheim, there is unfortunately very little to be found in the various reports, memoirs and the like about his work in the 'Academies', or symphony concerts. But these were only a sideline, so to speak. His main duties were at the opera house. Here he was in absolute charge of the repertoire and the cast of singers, and he could pick and choose which operas he wished to conduct himself. How he achieved all he did achieve is a minor miracle, for let us not forget that he came to Mannheim with practical experience of only two major operas: *Fidelio* and *Meistersinger*. Nor was he experienced on the managerial side. He was quite unfamiliar with the behind-the-scenes intrigues that seem to beset every opera house in the world, and we can see that his

31

days must have been full to excess. Moreover everyone had to contend with his 'stubbornness' and perfectionism. His refusal to compromise made life difficult at times for the *Intendant* of the Mannheim opera, Carl Hagemann, who wrote:

> Furtwängler is not a man of the theatre, neither in general as an organiser, nor in detail as an artist. He does have a sense of the theatre, but the theatre is not in his blood.

Furtwängler has been accused of approaching all operas symphonically. This is true only of Beethoven and Wagner. To a large extent their concept of opera and music drama stems from their inner symphonic sense. On the other hand Furtwängler approached Mozart's operas purely from the operatic standpoint and, at the risk of arousing a controversy, brought certain operatic overtones even to Mozart's symphonic music.

Furtwängler firmly believed that a conductor should know his scores from memory and *conduct* from memory, even if he had the score in front of him during the performance. In Mannheim he found himself a place to live where he was close to woods and open tracts of land, so that he could resume the solitary walking habits of his Strasbourg and Lübeck days, conducting and singing to himself. But, given all the circumstances, how else could he have managed? During these five years he mounted no less than 34 operas, 14 during his first season in 1915/16, four of which were new for Mannheim. He made his first appearance in September 1915 with *Fidelio* and in the course of time conducted every one of Wagner's works from *The Flying Dutchman* onwards (with the exception only of *Lohengrin*), as well as all the main Mozart operas, *Carmen*, two operas by Richard Strauss, Gluck's *Orpheus and Euridice*, *Der Freischütz*, and operas by Max von Schillings, his teacher, and Hans Pfitzner. It is interesting that his repertoire was chosen almost entirely from the German and Austrian operas. *Carmen* apart, he included no works by French composers, and Italian opera was represented only by Verdi's *Aida* and *Otello* and Rossini's *Barber of Seville*.

In Mannheim his conducting technique grew more assured, and as the years went by he became calmer: his aim was always to achieve a maximum of expression and musical effect, with a minimum of physical movement. Similarly he greatly reduced the amount of verbal instruction. Much later Frau Elisabeth Furtwängler was to write (p.37) that the words he used most often in rehearsal were 'Once more' or, pointing to his own hand, 'Once more – with me'. One is reminded of Knappertsbusch's reply to a young conductor who had asked him why he gave so few explanations to the orchestra in rehearsal: 'If I can't tell 'em with my stick, I can't tell 'em with my mouth!'

Another trait which became more pronounced in Furtwängler's character during the Mannheim period – and was to become even more so as time went on – was his sensitivity to all forms of criticism. In Lübeck he had been hailed unreservedly by press and audience alike, but in Mannheim standards were more critical. Hagemann writes:

> The newspapers especially could infuriate him, but as in general he had a good press there was really no reason for him to quarrel with the critics in the way, and to the extent, that was his custom. The slightest reproof, even if uttered in the most deferential manner, or a slightly different view in questions of interpretation could rob him of his equanimity and joy in music-making for days on end, and he often looked at me in amazement when I didn't attribute the least importance to negative opinions voiced by the press.

As the years went by, his name became known throughout Germany. This was mainly because in Mannheim he held a more prestigious position than in Lübeck, but geography may also account for it: Lübeck is in the extreme north of Germany, whereas Mannheim is centrally situated. During the Lübeck years Furtwängler only fulfilled one guest engagement of any importance: in June 1913 he was invited to conduct a concert in Vienna with the orchestra of the *Konzertverein*. This concert, for various reasons, was not much noticed, nor does Furtwängler himself seem to have found it particularly memorable, for when he returned to Vienna some years later and was asked by a journalist what he thought of the city he replied that he could not say much, as he had never been there before. It is true that, while still in Lübeck, he received a few invitations to Berlin, but he turned them all down as he did not want to go to the capital while he still felt inexperienced. Now that he was in Mannheim things were different, and he conducted his first concert in Berlin with the Philharmonic – an evening of Wagner and Richard Strauss – on 14 December 1917. Actually it was not much of a concert as far as Furtwängler was concerned. Mainly he had to accompany singers, and his own share of the evening consisted only of the *Tannhäuser* Overture and Strauss's *Don Juan*. Nevertheless the press notices the following day almost ignored the singers but praised the *Herr Hofkapellmeister* effusively – something that rarely happens in the Berlin press. Consequently he appeared again with the Philharmonic on three occasions in 1918, but the opportunities were necessarily limited since all the major concerts were in the hands of Nikisch. In February 1920 he scored a big success with a performance of Bruckner's Symphony No.8 which in those days was rarely played. (Incidentally in this concert he accompanied Edwin Fischer in Brahms's Piano Concerto No.2, which must have been the first time that these two musicians who were later to be such close friends worked together.) In April he conducted a special concert with the Berlin State Opera Orchestra, of which Richard Strauss was the principal conductor, and the following evening he performed Beethoven's Ninth with them. Strauss was already getting tired of this job, and Furtwängler was appointed his successor from the 1920/21 season onwards.

But it was not only Berlin which had attracted Furtwängler's attention. The *Tonkünstler-Orchester* in Vienna was without a conductor after Ferdinand Loewe's retirement, and in 1919 Furtwängler was contracted to conduct its regular as well as some of its special concerts, a position he held till 1924.[2] In 1921 he was appointed 'Concert Director' of the *Gesellschaft der Musikfreunde* in Vienna, which he remained for life.

Added to these obligations was another. Willem Mengelberg (1871-1951) was the permanent conductor of the well-known *Museumskonzerte* in Frankfurt, but he came to the conclusion that he was somewhat restricted there and wanted to make

---

[2] The *Tonkünstler-Orchester* and the orchestra of the *Konzertverein* were two independent bodies which, in about 1922, amalgamated to form the *Wiener Symphoniker*. As such they still exist as Vienna's second orchestra next to the Philharmonic. It must be stressed that, whereas the Philharmonic was, and is, in the main the orchestra of the Vienna State Opera, the *Symphoniker* are a purely symphonic ensemble without ties to any operatic institution.

more of an international career. In 1918/19 Furtwängler had already conducted some concerts in Frankfurt and, when Mengelberg resigned, he became his successor. Hamburg and Stockholm also wanted him, and he conducted in both cities several times – in Hamburg he was the principal conductor of the Fifth Brahms Festival. All attempts to put him under any permanent contract, however, were of no avail.

Clearly one man could not cope with this spate of engagements. With a feeling of sadness he resigned from his Mannheim position, his resignation taking effect at the end of the 1919/20 season. Sadness, because he was deprived for a while of conducting opera, which remained a great love of his to the end of his life. True, he continued to conduct opera and even had permanent positions in that field, but never again exclusively. After his move in 1920, Berlin remained his official residence until 1945.

In the 1920/21 season Furtwängler became a 'travelling conductor', who spent more time in trains and hotels than in his own home and, with short intervals, that was the way it was to remain. He had to fulfil his official duties in Berlin, Vienna and Frankfurt, and in addition he accepted guest engagements whenever his schedule allowed. Among the most important of these was an invitation to conduct the two 'special concerts' with the *Gewandhaus* Orchestra in 1921 on the occasion of the Leipzig Fair, both with the same programme. He was also engaged for a concert in the winter of 1921/22, as Nikisch had asked to tour South America with his pianist son Mitja (the first time in twenty-five years that Nikisch had asked for leave from a regular subscription concert of the *Gewandhaus*!) but through circumstances the engagement came to nothing.

Shortly afterwards Nikisch had to ask for leave of absence again. He had accepted an engagement to conduct in Holland on 26 January 1922, and the date clashed with one of the regular subscription concerts at the *Gewandhaus*. With Nikisch's consent, Furtwängler was invited to conduct in his stead, and the programme had already been agreed: Overture *Leonore II*, Brahms 'Haydn Variations' and the *Symphonie fantastique*. In the event, however, things turned out differently. After conducting a concert with his *Gewandhaus* Orchestra on 10

January 1922, Nikisch caught influenza. On the 23rd he died. Germany had lost its foremost conductor. Arriving in Leipzig on 24 January, Furtwängler immediately rang Max Brockhaus, a member of the directorate of the *Gewandhaus*. Brockhaus himself had only just been informed of Nikisch's death and imparted the sad news to him. The Nikisch family had suggested that the concert on the 26th should be cancelled, but this of course was impossible. Furtwängler agreed to alter the programme to consist of the *Coriolanus* Overture, Brahms's 'Four Serious Songs' and the *Eroica*, thus making it a true memorial concert. The Nikisch family objected that the last two movements of the *Eroica* were not suitable, and so in the end the first two items were retained and only the *Eroica* Funeral March, for which the whole of the audience stood – a fitting tribute to a great man. The programmes had already been printed but were reprinted. By some quirk of fate, however, only the first print has been preserved in the archives of the *Gewandhaus*, giving the *Eroica* as played complete.

After the concert the directors of the *Gewandhaus* agreed unanimously that Furtwängler should succeed Nikisch, and the decision was eventually ratified in April 1922 after some wrangling with the orchestra (according to Max Brockhaus). In Berlin Furtwängler also conducted a memorial concert, which also included the *Eroica*, and here again he was the natural choice as Nikisch's successor. He still had his official duties with the Berlin State Opera Orchestra, however, and it was inconceivable that one and the same person should be in charge of Berlin's two major subscription series of symphony concerts. But a formal request that he be relieved of his duties with the orchestra of the opera was readily granted, and Furtwängler took up the appointment with the Berlin Philharmonic. Apart from the two years immediately after the Second World War, he remained at its head until his death, but he relinquished his Leipzig position in 1928.

On 19 October 1922 Furtwängler's mother, whose greatest wish had always been to have a famous son, could proudly write in her diary:

Willi has Nikisch's post and is now probably in the highest position he can possibly attain.

4

Years of Fulfilment: 1922–1933

These eleven years must have been among the happiest in Furtwängler's life. As conductor and musical director of both the *Gewandhaus* and the Berlin Philharmonic he had reached eminence, an artistic greatness and acclaim, that were to be maintained for the rest of his life. In May 1922 he conducted the Vienna Philharmonic for the first time, the start of a life-long association with only a few interruptions. But what is more important, during those years he could be just a musician, just himself, untrammelled by political or other external considerations. True, he found little time to be creative as a composer, which bothered him, but in retrospect this was as nothing compared with the trials and tribulations which awaited him from 1933 onwards.

As the musical head of the two greatest orchestras in Germany, Furtwängler's renown rapidly spread through Europe. In 1924 he received his first invitation to conduct in England. His first appearance was in the Queen's Hall, London, on 24 January in a concert with the Royal Philharmonic Society Orchestra. This was followed by two further concerts with the London Symphony in February, and another one in November. He was acclaimed by the public and the press reception was favourable, though one critic said jocularly: 'Furtwängler will never go wrong so long as he sticks to symphonies in C minor' – for his first programme had included the Symphony No.1 by Brahms and the second Beethoven's Fifth. Even America became aware of him, and he was invited to conduct the New York Philharmonic in January 1925.

He arrived in New York in December 1924 and spent Christmas there. His first concert was in Carnegie Hall on 3 January 1925 with Casals as soloist, and it was an almost unparalleled success. The audience – probably the most demanding he had faced since his first appearances in Berlin – went mad, and the reviewers were full of praise, even Olin Downes, America's foremost music critic. It was to remain that way for the other eleven concerts he conducted during his visit, including his last appearance on 30 January 1925, and he returned to Europe well pleased that he had conquered New York. This was to some extent a miscalculation, however, for he was ignorant of the quite different composition of the American musical scene. Accustomed to municipal or state-supported orchestras, he was unfamiliar with the privately subsidised American orchestras with their committees of wealthy citizens and society politics. In this world it was simply not possible for him to refuse an invitation to a reception given by the New York élite in order to spend an evening in the company of musicians to talk music. Furtwängler, true to his own self, acted and behaved in the manner he was accustomed to, and did not realise how many enemies he made. Therefore, while his second visit in early 1926 was no less fervently acclaimed by the general public, there was a distinctly lukewarm feeling in the press and in certain sections of American high society, and he was somewhat bewildered. On his third visit, in early 1927, there was a further factor. The Chairman of the Philharmonic Board, Clarence H. Mackay, had been anxious for some time to obtain the services of Toscanini, and had succeeded for the 1926/27 season. It was the first time that Furtwängler had become so directly involved with politics. At this point it was still a question only of 'musical' politics, and let it be stressed that in those days the relationship between Furtwängler and Toscanini was still perfectly harmonious from the musical point of view – Toscanini attended a Furtwängler concert, Furtwängler went to Toscanini's rehearsals. The political ructions between the two were to come much later. But in the circles that mattered in New York in early 1927 this became an 'issue'. Olin Downes sided with Toscanini, and Furtwängler found that he did not have a single friend on the Board of the Philharmonic. True, he won ovations from his public, and even Downes had to pay grudging tribute to his performance of Brahms's 'German Requiem', the last concert he was to conduct in North America. But he left the country on 7 April 1927 as a humiliated, exasperated and disillusioned man. He was never to set foot in North America again.[1]

On his return Furtwängler found little time to nurse his grievances. There was his work with the Berlin Philharmonic and the *Gewandhaus*, and there were guest engagements in various towns, either by himself or with his orchestras. The most notable town was probably Heidelberg, where he conducted three concerts in June 1927, for in that year the world was commemorating the centenary of Beethoven's death. He was awarded an honorary doctorate. This always remained for him the greatest honour he ever received. True, in subsequent years further honours were conferred on him. On 29 May 1929 he was elected to the *Friedensklasse des Pour le mérite*.[2] In 1932 he won the Goethe Medal, and in 1939 he was made a commander of the *Légion d'honneur*. He was gratified by all these honours, but the one he valued most – and the only one he ever made use of – was his Heidelberg doctorate. He was never known as *'Generalmusikdirektor'*, 'Professor', let alone *'Staatsrat'* (a title given him as a sop by the Nazis). Nobody would have recognised him by these titles. But if you addressed him personally you called him *'Herr Doktor'*, and if, out of earshot, you spoke of *'Der Doktor'* everyone in the musical world knew immediately whom you meant.

This Heidelberg episode, however, was an isolated event. In that year, 1927, more was to follow to fill his life even more. Felix Weingartner (1863-1942), who had held sway over the Vienna Philharmonic for so many years, decided to retire and live in Switzerland. A successor had to be found. There was no question: Furtwängler was their man. He accepted the appointment, which he retained until 1930. In the autumn of

---

[1] In 1926 and 1927 Furtwängler also conducted concerts with the New York Philharmonic (to whom he was under exclusive contract) in Philadelphia, Washington, Baltimore, Pittsburgh, Harrisburg and Reading.

[2] The *Pour le mérite* had been instituted as a military and civilian award by Frederick the Great and represented the highest possible honour that could be bestowed on anyone in Prussia. In 1842 an equivalent for the Arts and Sciences was created, the so-called 'Peace Class' of the *Pour le mérite*.

1927 he conducted the first of the Philharmonic Concerts in Vienna in his official capacity. For the 1927/28 season he was the Chief Conductor both of the Berlin and of the Vienna Philharmonic Orchestras, as well as of the Leipzig *Gewandhaus*, the three top-ranking orchestras of Germany and Austria. It was a position of power that no conductor has held before or since. His energies were stretched to the utmost. He was continually travelling from one town to the other, and in the 1927/28 season he conducted no less than 118 concerts. He himself realised that the situation was impossible, and that he was unfair to the demands of the time-honoured traditions of Leipzig. He resigned and left the *Gewandhaus* in 1928. The irony is that in the following 1928/29 season he conducted even more concerts – 127 in all!

*

We must now look at another aspect of Furtwängler's work, namely his orchestral tours. The Board of the *Gewandhaus* had always been reluctant to let its orchestra travel abroad. In fact in 1913 they had turned down the offer of a major tour of South America. Then, at long last, Nikisch had persuaded them, and in 1916 and 1917 they visited Switzerland, their first appearances outside Germany. It was with the *Gewandhaus*, in 1923, that Furtwängler undertook his first tour abroad at the head of one of his orchestras. Again they visited Switzerland. We have seen already that Furtwängler had been in England on his own as a guest conductor in 1924, in January/February and November, but symphony orchestras still did not travel the globe in those days. In 1924, to strengthen its shaky finances, the Berlin Philharmonic decided to tour within Germany and even occasionally in Switzerland. The venture paid off and became a regular routine. It was now that Berta Geissmar, with her undoubted organising genius, came into her own. According to her memoirs, it was she who first suggested that the Berlin Philharmonic should visit England. The idea was favourably received, and it was left to her to make the arrangements. Although she was a good organiser, and even a good representative, she was also at times somewhat lacking in diplomacy, to Furtwängler's occasional disadvantage. Neverthe-less, in general she was successful, and in December 1927 the Berlin Philharmonic went on its first tour to England with Furtwängler, giving two concerts in London and one in Manches-ter. They were widely acclaimed and set the pace for regular return visits in the winter months of most succeeding years: in November 1928, December 1929, March 1931, February 1932, February 1933, January 1934, November/December 1935 and January 1938, and also in May 1937 during the Coronation. The Second World War put an end to this happy musical contact, and Furtwängler did not conduct in England again until 1948. Before the war, apart from London and Manchester, the Berlin Phil-harmonic in Britain under Furtwängler was heard in Liverpool, Bristol, Birmingham, Sheffield, Newcastle, Edinburgh, Glasgow, Dundee and Brighton. In April 1930 Furtwängler also visited England with the Vienna Philharmonic. This may have been a special gesture to that orchestra, for he was about to break his contractual relationship with them. He did not return to Britain with the Vienna Philharmonic until after 1947. In his connections with England it is worth noting that he first conducted at Covent Garden in May 1935, giving two performances of *Tristan und Isolde*, and two *Ring* cycles at the Royal Opera in May/June 1937, during the Coronation season, in co-operation with Sir Thomas Beecham.

In France matters took a similar course. Furtwängler first appeared in Paris with the Berlin Philharmonic in the spring of 1928. On this first visit they played in the *Salle Pleyel*, but in later years in the *Opéra*. These spring concerts became almost annual events. They visited Paris again in 1930, 1932, 1933, 1934, 1937 and 1938, and also travelled to other major cities, notably to Lyons and Marseille. From 1932 Furtwängler became a regular guest in May or June at the *Opéra* in Paris, where he invariably conducted Wagner. These came to be known as the 'Furtwängler-Wagner' seasons, and in June 1938 Furwängler conducted the 100th Paris performance of *Tristan und Isolde*.[3] In Paris and other French cities he had an enthusiastic following, and his

[3] Some sources give 1937 as the date of this performance of *Tristan*, but the *Bibliothèque de l'Opéra*, Paris, has confirmed to me that it took place on 21 June 1938.

audiences gratefully acknowledged that he refused to visit France again during the war years, just as he refused to visit any other country subjugated by the Nazis.

While it was in England and France that the regular tours were made, other countries were not neglected. Between 1927 and 1936 they visited Denmark, Holland, Luxembourg, Belgium, Poland and Czechoslovakia, and in 1931/32 they travelled to Italy for the first time. Of course, Furtwängler had a soft spot for Italy, dating back to his boyhood, and it is perhaps symptomatic that, after those two years 1945-47 when he was barred, it was in Italy – in Rome and Florence – that he first conducted again.

In these years another difficult decision awaited him. During the 1928/29 season the Vienna State Opera invited him for the first time as a guest conductor. Previously he had only appeared in Vienna as a conductor of symphony concerts. He made his Viennese opera debut with *Rheingold*. It was the last season of Franz Schalk (1863-1931) as musical director, and a successor had to be found. Not unnaturally everyone opted for Furtwängler. He was in a quandary. On the one hand he loved the *ambience* of Vienna, both from the personal and from the musical point of view. His widow endearingly recalls how, on the journey from Berlin to Vienna, he tried to suppress his Berlin accent and practised a Viennese inflection. Moreover his love of opera had always remained with him, and here, for the first time since Mannheim, he could be at the head of an opera house – perhaps the finest in the world. On the other hand there was also his beloved Berlin Philharmonic to consider. Its finances were at their lowest ebb, so that the very existence of the orchestra was seriously threatened. After many discussions a *modus operandi* was agreed upon. The orchestra was to become a limited company, with the 95 orchestra members, the German State and the town of Berlin in partnership. It would receive a guaranteed annual subsidy of 480,000 marks, of which Berlin had to pay 75 per cent, the remainder being borne by the German Government and the State of Prussia. There was one condition: Furtwängler must remain in charge as Musical Director and Conductor and sign a ten-year contract. We shall never know what heart-ache it was to Furtwängler to make his decision. It must have seemed an incredible responsibility. In the end he decided in favour of Berlin. The orchestra, which meant so much to him, was saved. They have never forgotten what it meant to them, or what a personal sacrifice he made. They stood by him through all adversities to the end. In consequence the town of Berlin appointed him *Städtischer Generalmusikdirektor* ('Municipal director of Music'). In Vienna, on the other hand, where he had already been 'Concert Director' of the *Gesellschaft der Musikfreunde* since 1921 – an appointment he retained till his death – the refusal was taken very much amiss. There is and always had been a rivalry, though beneath the surface, between Berlin and Vienna.

Another problem was Bayreuth. On 4 August 1930 Siegfried Wagner died. After Richard Wagner's death his wife Cosima had taken over direction of the Bayreuth Festival, and their son Siegfried had succeeded her. His wife Winifred now became the mistress of Bayreuth, but someone had to be found with the necessary musicianship and knowledge to succeed him. Winifred Wagner approached Furtwängler in late 1930 and offered him the conductorship and entire artistic direction of the Festival – a position that no one had held in Bayreuth since Wagner. Furtwängler accepted. He and Toscanini were to be the two chief conductors at the 1931 Bayreuth season. In those days it was customary for each Bayreuth Festival to include *Parsifal*, the *Ring* and one or two other Wagner operas. It should also be noted that there were gaps in the Bayreuth seasons. They took place annually only from 1936 to 1944, and then again from 1951.

In 1930 Toscanini was the first non-German to be invited to conduct Wagner in Bayreuth. In that year he conducted *Tristan* and *Tannhäuser*, and in 1931 *Parsifal* and again *Tannhäuser*. For Furtwängler, 1931 was his first year in Bayreuth, and he directed three performances of *Tristan*. It is no secret that Frau Winifred Wagner was very difficult to get on with, and there were ructions with both Furtwängler and Toscanini. It must be stressed that in those days all these differences were of a personal, not a political nature. That Winifred Wagner was a fanatical Nazi even then and a close personal friend of Hitler was not yet a factor. Both Furtwängler and Toscanini left

Bayreuth, vowing never to return; and so Bayreuth, which had just had the two greatest living conductors at the helm, suddenly found itself without either. The story goes that Frau Winifred subsequently reconciled Toscanini; but this is of no great importance, for there was no Bayreuth season in 1932, and by 1933 Hitler had appeared on the scene. This automatically meant that Toscanini would not return, and he never conducted in Bayreuth again. Furtwängler, however, conducted Wagner again on the *Grüne Hügel* (the 'Green Hill', as the Festival Theatre was called) in 1936, 1937, 1943 and 1944. After the war he conducted Beethoven's Ninth in the memorable performance of 29 July 1951, on the occasion of the re-inauguration of the Bayreuth Festivals, and again on 9 August 1954 in what may be called his farewell to Bayreuth.

There is no need to enumerate all Furtwängler's professional activities during this period. Suffice it to say that he travelled widely in Europe as a guest conductor and was for a short period the conductor of the Municipal Opera in Berlin-Charlottenburg. A highlight was the concert of 15 April 1932 on the occasion of the fiftieth anniversary of the Berlin Philharmonic, when he gave the first performance of Hindemith's Philharmonic Concerto (dedicated to him and the Berlin Philharmonic) and received the Goethe Medal, a coveted prize for services in the field of the Arts and Sciences first awarded in 1927.

*

But in the midst of these professional activities Furtwängler also managed to lead a private life. Berlin, to which he had moved in 1920, became his domicile until 1945, when he made his permanent home in Switzerland; but even so he retained a residence in Berlin to the day of his death. In 1920 he acquired a treasure in the person of Helene Matschenz, the faithful and devoted housekeeper who looked after him to the end. Frau Helene – or 'Lenchen', as she was generally known – was a typical Berlin woman, though she was not actually born there. For anyone familiar with the life of Bruckner, there is a distinct parallel between Helene Matschenz and Bruckner's house-keeper Katharina Kachelmayr, 'Frau Kathi'. 'Lenchen' soon took over completely. Though she always called him *Herr Doktor*, when referring to him to anybody else he was always *Der Meester* ('the Master', prounced in broad Berlinese). Apart from his second wife Elisabeth, there was probably no one who understood him better: his ways, his likes and dislikes, *what* he liked and *when*. She ruled him with a gentle and adoring tyranny. She also knew with utter conviction whom *she* liked and disliked, and made no bones about it. Everyone in Furtwängler's circle, whether personal or professional, did his best to get into her good books. Frau Elisabeth told me that when she married Furtwängler she was mightily worried that 'Lenchen might not approve of her', and understandably was much relieved to hear that Lenchen had remarked to him: *Ik find' Se hamm in'n joldenen Pott jefasst!* ('I think you have found her in a pot of gold'). Later Lenchen even allowed Frau Elisabeth to come into her kitchen and do some cooking in her own home!

Another woman of importance in Furtwängler's life was his first wife Zitla Lund, a Dane, about whom we know relatively little. She was two years older and had been married twice before. They were married on 22 May 1923. She appears to have been witty, vivacious and elegant, but these appearances were deceptive, for she had no real brains.[4] It is not surprising, therefore, that the marriage (which remained childless) was not successful, for the highly cultured Furtwängler only liked the company of people with whom he could discuss music, art and philosophy. Moreover, she tried to teach Furtwängler how to conduct, and was critical of everything he or his soloists did. Two stories will suffice. Erna Berger describes how Furtwängler, on the podium, appeared to her

> ...transfigured, and the radiance of that divine music enveloped us all. He looked like an archangel! But during intermission, this 'archangel' became a little boy being scolded... Furtwängler was 'advised' on conducting by his wife Zitla, and my husband tried to explain to me how I could best interpret the music! This occasion struck us as funny, and we often laughed about it in later years.

Frau Elisabeth herself told me a story of how in June 1943 in Zürich after a rehearsal for *Siegfried* they were all three having

---

[4] From here on for convenience I shall refer to the first Mrs Furtwängler as 'Frau Zitla' and the second as 'Frau Elisabeth'.

lunch and he asked Frau Zitla with a grin: 'Now tell me, which of the singers was the worst?'

When they were married they lived near the Tiergarten in Berlin, and in the winter of 1923 Furtwängler bought a holiday house near St Moritz. Again it is typical that he did not wish to live in the fashionable part of the resort but chose a place where he had the forest on his doorstep and could indulge in those long walks which meant so much to him. They soon began to go their separate ways. She seems to have spent much of her time in the country house, for Furtwängler in letters to friends made remarks like: 'I spent a few days with Zitla in St Moritz.' He owned this house right up to his death, and it is still owned by Frau Elisabeth.

In the early 1930s Furtwängler decided that the time had come for him to live on his own again, but of course the faithful Lenchen moved with him. He had found a first-floor apartment in the *Fasanerie* in the *Wildpark* (Deer Park) in Potsdam, once again in a place where he could walk and indulge in sports such as riding. As the whole area round Sanssouci is state-owned property, he could not buy it. In any case in those days such a thing as 'buying a flat' was hardly known. The *Fasanerie* remained his private address until after the war, although he was not often at home. Nor was there much time for composing. The only composition he wrote was a Piano Quintet, which he first mentions in a letter of 1915. Autograph sketches date from 1924, and it was finished in 1934, though there is no evidence that the work was performed.

There is another personal aspect of Furtwängler's life that we cannot ignore. On the one hand, as we have noted about his Lübeck days, he always seems to have remained a 'grown-up boy'. This could not fail to arouse motherly feelings in women slightly older than himself. There was a change only in the early 1930s when he was in his mid-forties. On the other hand there is no denying that a performing musician, particularly a conductor, exudes a mysterious attraction for women. Be that as it may, Furtwängler was no saint, and by the time he married Frau Zitla he was already the proud father of three children, all from illicit love affairs: Wilhelm (born 1916), Dagmar (born 1920) and Friederike (born about 1921). A few months after his marriage in 1923 he had a fourth child, Iva. In 1934, he had another daughter, Almut, with the actress Irme Schwab. With the consent of Frau Zitla he had already officially adopted his son Wilhelm and the daughter Friederike. His relationship with all five children remained ideal to the end, for he adored children. Apart from Irme Schwab, all their mothers were older than himself, and it is a heart-warming token of human understanding and feeling that to this day Frau Elisabeth remains in close touch with all five children, as well as with Irme Schwab.

5

The Nazis: 1933–1939

On 30 January 1933 Adolf Hitler came to power. During the preceding years there had already been ominous pointers, but few people inside or outside Germany had taken the threat seriously, and even now most of them considered it a passing phase. Few realised that, when propounding his mad ideas, Hitler meant exactly what he said and had every intention of putting them into practice. In the fourteen years since the end of the First World War Germany had lived under the so-called Weimar Republic, had had no less than eight general elections and had seen fourteen Chancellors. So it is not surprising, and I still remember it, that one heard the opinion expressed: 'Why not give Hitler a chance – if we don't like him, we can always throw him out.' I am proud to say that my own father was far-sighted enough, as early as 1930/31, to say: 'If you let that fellow in, you'll never get rid of him again.'

Then, in January 1933, the Nazi terror began, at first on a small scale, but the ferocity increased year by year. The Nazis pursued their policies with German efficiency and in absolute secrecy, and I know very well – though many will not believe it even now – that the vast majority of ordinary Germans barely knew of the existence of concentration camps, let alone of the horrors perpetrated in them. But we are not so much concerned with these extremes. What is more relevant is that the whole of Germany was in fact one huge concentration camp. The Gestapo was Big Brother watching everyone. Denunciation was rife and encouraged by the powers-that-be.

I have gone into these matters at some length on purpose, for it is more than forty years since the 'Thousand Year *Reich*' came to its inglorious end, so that the percentage of those who have first-hand knowledge of Germany during those crucial twelve years between 1933 and 1945 is ever dwindling. When we come to speak of the open letter that Furtwängler wrote to Goebbels in 1933, or the passionate defence of Hindemith he published in the press in 1934, young persons today, accustomed to the democratic liberties of the western world, may shrug their shoulders and say to themselves: 'So what? He just wrote a couple of letters to *The Times!*', little realising that in doing what he did Furtwängler risked his freedom, even his life. The crux of the matter is that Furtwängler was a person of the utmost integrity with strong feelings of moral responsibility, and that he felt himself totally as a German musician – not as belonging to the Germany of Hitler and his minions, but to the Germany of Bach and Beethoven, of Goethe and Schiller, of Schopenhauer and Kant.

In the context of Furtwängler and the Hitler regime we must go back to Furtwängler's differences with Winifred Wagner which led, in the spring of 1932, to his resignation as artistic director of the Bayreuth Festival. Naturally the question of his successor was actively debated in artistic circles, and on 26 June 1932 the *Deutsche Allgemeine Zeitung* published an article devoted to the problem. Two days later Furtwängler took the drastic step of writing an article in reply under the heading *Um die Zukunft von Bayreuth* ('Regarding the Future of Bayreuth') which was published in the same daily. We need not go into all the details. Suffice it to say that he stated categorically that his resignation had nothing to do with Toscanini, and that his differences with Winifred Wagner were about who was to have the final authority in artistic decisions. Shortly after, in summer 1932, Furtwängler met Hitler for the first time and had a conversation with him in the Hotel Kaiserhof in Berlin. Now it so happened that Furtwängler had better things to do with his time than to read newspapers, let alone listen to political broadcasts, and so, in those days when everyone was discussing political events, for him Hitler was just a name. Hitler must have read or heard about Furtwängler's Bayreuth article, and he immediately turned to that subject, telling him that he was not doing the right thing and explaining how he, Hitler the great Wagnerian, envisaged the future of Bayreuth. Much later, according to Riess (p.129), Furtwängler commented on this encounter: 'He talked about questions regarding Bayreuth ... That man had a number of wayward and rather conventional ideas about art. His lack of artistic standards would have frightened me, had I not been sure at the time that Hitler would never come to power!' Riess (p.131) also tells how, shortly after, Furtwängler talked to André François-Poncet, the French Ambassador to Berlin. François-Poncet asked him: 'You have spoken to him?' Furtwängler countered cautiously with the question: 'Do you know him?' François-Poncet smiled: 'Yes, I have met him. A strange man. He appeared to me like a cross between Joan of Arc and Charlie Chaplin!... And what impression has Mr Hitler made on you?' Furtwängler replied: 'He ...? Actually no impression at all.'

Furtwängler always believed – and in the years to come had to battle for his belief – that politics was the business of politicians and music of musicians, and that the two had nothing in common. Heads of state and their governments might have their private opinions, their personal likes and dislikes, for whatever reasons, but the idea that an artist might therefore be proscribed, or the theatre of a great director like Max Reinhardt closed down, was unthinkable. All this changed in the twinkling of an eye when Hitler and his brown hordes took over – for they took over everything, including the whole field of art and cultural life of which they were completely ignorant.

On that famous 30 January 1933, one of the most decisive dates in modern history (not only for Germany, but for the whole world), Furtwängler was abroad with the Berlin Philharmonic touring Holland, Belgium and Great Britain. He returned three weeks later, and even he could not help noticing the winds of change. The first manifestations were more irritating than anything else. Party officials called on Furtwängler. They wrote to him and rang him up, all urging him to replace the Jewish musicians in his orchestra and in particular to get rid of his secretary Berta Geissmar. All this annoyed Furtwängler, but he ignored it. Then came the great exodus. Men of outstanding talent such as Bruno Walter and Klemperer, Schnabel and

Huberman, Max Reinhardt and many others emigrated.

The case of Bruno Walter is worth a special mention as it caused the greatest stir outside Germany. Walter, then the chief conductor of the *Gewandhaus* in succession to Furtwängler, had long been a welcome guest in Europe and the United States. He too was out of Germany, conducting in America, when Hitler assumed power. He was informed of events by the press and looked to the future with trepidation. Nevertheless he returned to Germany in March 1933, as he had to conduct a *Gewandhaus* subscription concert. The moment he arrived in Berlin he was called to Leipzig for a consultation with Max Brockhaus, one of the *Gewandhaus* Directors. Brockhaus told him that the police wanted to stop his concert. Walter offered to resign to avoid trouble, but Brockhaus advised him to stand his ground: 'Once you give in to these fellows, everything is lost.' Nevertheless, when he arrived for the public rehearsal on the morning of the concert he found the doors of the *Gewandhaus* locked and a poster announcing that the concert would not take place. In the artists' room he found a dejected Board of Directors. Little was said. There was not much one could say. As they shook hands and said farewell, they all knew that something irreparable had happened.

Deeply apprehensive, Walter returned to Berlin the same day. On the following Monday he was supposed to conduct a concert in the series of 'Bruno Walter Concerts' which were organised by Louise Wolff. He went to see her and learnt that the Ministry of Propaganda, without actually banning the concert, had informed her that, if it took place as planned, they would see to it that everything in the hall would be smashed and suggested that she find a substitute conductor. When she was unable to find anyone ready to stab a friend and colleague in the back, the Ministry suggested Richard Strauss. Strauss agreed and conducted in Bruno Walter's stead.[1] By then Walter had left Germany for Austria. By the time he arrived there the whole

---

[1] These are the facts as they have generally been accepted. However, it should be mentioned that in May 1955 the Richard Strauss Society in their *Mitteilungsblätter* gave the full text of a letter from the surviving daughter of Louise Wolff addressed to the son of Richard Strauss. According to this, Strauss was at first unwilling to take over the direction of the concert; but apparently it was Bruno Walter himself who, before leaving Berlin, expressed the wish that Strauss should replace him.

affair had been reported in the international press. As a result, within 48 hours Bruno Walter received so many invitations to come as a guest conductor that he was fully booked up for the next two years. Wherever he went in the following months he was greeted with ovations. Naturally they were for him as the great musician that he was, but there was a distinct political undercurrent. They were also a demonstration of the free world against the Nazi dictatorship.

It was at this juncture that Furtwängler decided to take a hand. He said himself that he had already been upset by the defamation to which excellent artists of Jewish origin had been subjected; but the ban on the 'Bruno Walter Concerts' had infuriated him to such an extent that he could no longer remain silent, and in April 1933 he wrote a letter to Goebbels, the Minister of Propaganda, who was also in charge of everything to do with the theatre and music.[2] In it he stressed that he was writing purely in his capacity as an artist and recognised only the divide between good and bad art. He agreed that one should fight against worthless music, irrespective of whether it was by Jewish or non-Jewish composers, but that the world crisis in the musical life of the day could not stand any more experiments and could not forego the services of true artists. He concluded:

> It must be said quite clearly that men like Walter, Klemperer, Reinhardt, etc. must also in future have their artistic say in Germany.
> I repeat: our fight must be directed against the unnatural, shallow and destructive spirit, but not against the real artist who, in whatever way and however one may evaluate his art, is formative and as such creative.
> This is why I appeal to you in the name of German art to prevent things happening which are irrevocable.

I very much doubt whether Furtwängler was aware that this letter constituted a declaration of war. Even the moves and actions of powerful men like Goebbels and Göring were subject to Hitler's approval. So, in a way, in disagreeing with Goebbels's policies he was indirectly attacking Hitler himself, and that simply would not do. After all the motto of the day was *Der Führer hat immer recht!* ('The *Führer* is always right!'). On receiving the letter, Goebbels rang Furtwängler and asked

---

[2] The complete text of this letter can be found in Riess (p. 142/3) and elsewhere.

affably if he could publish the letter in the daily press. Furtwängler gladly agreed, for he thought the public at large would thus be informed of his views. Little did he realise that Goebbels was only too glad to print his own reply alongside. With all the propagandistic wiles at his command, Goebbels stressed in his reply that politics were also an art, that music and politics could not be separated, and that it was a national duty to eradicate 'foreign' (i.e. Jewish) elements to open the path for all those artists who had been ignored and suppressed during the years of the Weimar Republic.

But the Bruno Walter affair had another consequence. Goebbels must have been highly perturbed by the reaction to Walter's emigration in the outside world, and he saw clearly that if Furtwängler too was to leave Germany he would be received everywhere with equally open arms. This had to be prevented at all costs for, as the foremost conductor of Germany, Furtwängler with his enormous international prestige was an object of nationalistic cultural propaganda for Goebbels and his Ministry. Goebbels therefore gave instructions that Furtwängler was to be treated with kid gloves and not be antagonised in any way whatsoever. Unfortunately, as we shall see, this raised in Furtwängler during the next eighteen months the false hope that he was steering the Nazis into more moderate channels, and that everything might still turn out for the best. It has been said that Furtwängler was politically naive. When it came to Nazi machinations he was as defenceless as a babe facing a pack of wolves, especially when they donned their sheep's clothing for his benefit.

*

The question has often been asked: why did Furtwängler stay in Germany? It has sometimes been suggested that he was loth to relinquish the powerful position he held – in other words that he was acting for purely selfish reasons. This surely cannot be true if we consider the never-ending troubles he had to go through during the Hitler regime, these constant battles, when he must have known very well that he could have built up an easy life for himself by emigrating, which would have proved to be rewarding personally, artistically and financially. No: the truth can only be found in Furtwängler's own character. First, his whole being, his heart and soul, had its roots in German art and culture. Secondly he was dominated by a feeling of moral responsibility and a duty to help wherever he could. We must not forget that of all the artists who left Germany between 1933 and 1939 (and after 1938 also Austria and the other territories annexed by Hitler) the vast majority left for racial reasons. It may be cruel to say this, but for them it was relatively easy to come to a decision. Basically it was a choice between life and death, between emigrating into freedom or being sent to a concentration camp. On the other hand there were other artists who, in Nazi terms, were 'Aryan' and for whom therefore the decision was not one of such drastic consequence. I am thinking here, among others, of the conductor Fritz Busch and his violinist brother Adolf, of Erich Kleiber, and of Thomas Mann. They simply reached their own conclusions from what they saw happening around them and decided that they could no longer live under such a despicable system, and that they preferred to leave their homeland in order to breathe freely. Furtwängler was of a different opinion and this is perhaps best expressed in two diary entries which he made in 1945 and 1946 respectively:

All those who became emigrants or demanded that one should emigrate have relieved Hitler of having to prove one thing: his claim that he was the true representative of the German nation. They thought that one *had* to leave a Nazi Germany, but just this is wrong. Germany never *was* a Nazi Germany, but a Germany subjugated by the Nazis.

I have tried to examine myself very conscientiously. I am no better than others, but I must say what my own instinct was. And there are two things: love for my country and my people, which is a physical and spiritual matter; and a feeling of being given a task to alleviate injustice. The battle for the soul of the German nation is only fought here [in Germany]. From outside one can only voice protests – anyone can do that.

Many people have misunderstood this attitude and will do so to this day, and many of his personal friends and colleagues from all over the world urged him to leave Germany. But others saw his point and, after the famous letter to Goebbels was

The ancestral homestead in the Black Forest

Wilhelm's parents

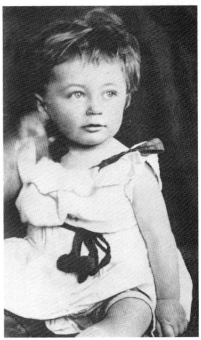

Wilhelm as a baby

Walter, Märit and Wilhelm with their parents

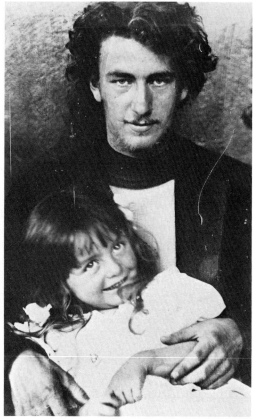

With Ludwig Curtius   With his youngest sister Annele

The country house *Tanneck* (Wilhelm far right)

With friends by the lake (Wilhelm far right)

In Zürich, 1906/7   In Lübeck, *c.* 1912

With Märit, Annele and Walter in the 1914-18 War

In the 1920s

The *Fasanerie* in Potsdam

At his piano

Concert with the Berlin Philharmonic in the *Palais des Beaux Arts,* Brussels

Above and left:
Rehearsing the Vienna
Philharmonic

The Chalet in St Moritz

Above: In St Moritz with his first wife Zitla

Left: In St Moritz with his mother

In the mountains with
Klemperer

Riding (Photo: AP)

On a picnic

Skiing (Photo: Lothar Rübelt)

On Lake Geneva: concentrating
intensely on a score . . .

. . . until a pretty lady comes along!

With the Berlin Philharmonic in the *Titania-Palast*, 1947

Beethoven's Ninth in Bayreuth, 1954

In rehearsal. The relaxed left arm with a loosely clenched fist was a typical gesture (Photo: Hubert Spies, Frankfurt)

With Sibelius, 1950 (Photo: Hede Foto)

With Menuhin in Lucerne, 1947

With his wife Elisabeth and the
Kokoschkas in Salzburg, 1954
(Photo: H. Hagen, Salzburg)

With Frau Elisabeth in Paris, 1954

With his son Andreas in Salzburg, 1954

In the garden, his left hand caressing a flower as it caressed beautiful sounds from his orchestras

Villa Le Basset-Coulon, Clarens

At Badgastein, six weeks
before he died.

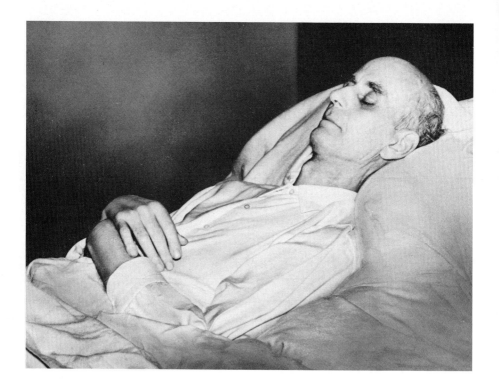

Frau Elisabeth writes: 'This photo was taken one or two hours after he died, still on his death bed, in one of his rehearsal shirts, his hands as I placed them. Truly: Death and Transfiguration'

reprinted everywhere, Furtwängler received letters and tele-grams from far and wide, congratulating him and confirming him in his decision. When Max Reinhardt left Germany, his closest associate and collaborator Clemens Herzberg (also Jewish) accompanied him to Cherbourg. Reinhardt's last words to Herz-berg were: 'When you get back to Berlin, give Furtwängler my regards and tell him that he is doing the right thing by remaining in Germany.'[3] Herzberg, incidentally, stayed for the duration of the Third *Reich*, much of the time in hiding, and became one of the key witnesses for the defence when Furtwängler had to undergo a denazification trial after the war.

Another refugee from Furtwängler's circle who supported him in his decision was Arnold Schönberg. His wife remembers:

> In Paris, 1933, [Furtwängler] came to our hotel and offered to negotiate with the German authorities on our behalf. How different from Richard Strauss's ironic reply to Otto Klemperer, 'Just the right moment to intervene for a Jew!'
>
> Furtwängler knew that the Germans had done a terrible wrong to Schönberg and he suffered for it as a German, and felt it his duty to interfere. Not only as a musician but also as a friend. But the most remarkable moment came when he, more desperate than Schönberg, cried out: 'What shall I do now?' Arnold told him: 'You have to stay and conduct good music.' He did, and whatever trick was used to soil his name, instigating a whisper campaign and later a very loud one: *he never was a Nazi*.

So Furtwängler continued his lone battle for justice in the midst of the evil forces by which he was surrounded. There are innumerable accounts of how he tried to help both in small ways and large, sparing no time, trouble or inconvenience if he could be of any assistance. In 1979, in a television documentary about Furtwängler and the politics of the Hitler era, a journalist interviewed Boleslaw Barlog, one of the leading figures in Berlin's theatrical life since the 1930s, himself an ardent anti-Nazi, and asked him whether he could name anyone whom Furtwängler had assisted, to which Barlog replied: 'Look, there were so many of them – hundreds. You can't expect me to remember names.' To cite but one example of Furtwängler's

---

[3] So according to Riess (p. 155). According to Gillis, *Furtwängler and America* (p. 84), Reinhardt said these words to Herzberg at a meeting in Paris in 1933.

genuine kindness, I quote from Riess (p.149) the words of one of the first violins of the Berlin Philharmonic Orchestra:

> Furtwängler's interest for the orchestra went far beyond the purely artistic. He was our benefactor! What did he not do to save those who were endangered! My wife is Jewish ... When my son wanted to marry, Furtwängler went from pillar to post to get the necessary permission. He said: 'My dear Wolff, your boy is also one of us.' ... The words he used against the Hitler regime! Every single sentence could have cost him his life.

If I may be allowed to tell a personal story, in the early 1950s I was talking to someone fairly high up in the music department of the BBC. He told me that after 1933 many musicians arrived with letters of recommendation from Furtwängler. After a while they just ignored them: they came to realise that whenever a musician was forced to leave Germany for political or racial reasons Furtwängler would give him a glowing letter of introduction irrespective of whether he was good, bad or indifferent as a musician – just to help him.

All this concerns individuals, as does Furtwängler's tremendous courage in defending his secretary Berta Geissmar, until at last she, too, in December 1935, was forced to emigrate, first to America and then to England. But his greatest battle, not unnaturally, was directed to the retention and protection of the Jewish members of his own orchestra. His only safeguard lay in his national and international prestige, and under this shield he took risks by word and action which would have meant a death sentence for any ordinary German. For instance, long before the advent of Hitler, it had been agreed with Mannheim (a town for which, as we have seen, he had a special affection and where he enjoyed the Freedom of the City) that, in the spring of 1933, the Mannheim Orchestra and the Berlin Philharmonic would combine for a concert under Furtwängler's direction, the profits to go to the funds of the Mannheim Orchestra. Furtwängler had stipulated that his own concert master Szymon Goldberg should be the leader of the combined forces. As the political climate by now had changed, the members of the Mannheim orchestra committee insisted that their own concert master should sit in that position, even though he was vastly inferior – but their man was a member of the Nazi party, whereas Goldberg was Jewish.

Furtwängler, however, remained adamant and threatened to cancel the whole concert if he did not have his way. He also insisted that he would bring his whole orchestra, including the Jewish members. The concert duly took place, but during the interval members of the Mannheim committee came to the artists' room and accused him of 'lack of national feeling'. That was just the sort of thing to say to Furtwängler! He flew into a rage, threw at their feet a score he had just been reading and shouted *'Get out!'* Even before the Mannheim committee members could beat a retreat he tried to rush from the room, and it was only at his own orchestra's persuasion that the second half of the concert took place.

After the concert there was to be a big banquet in honour of Furtwängler and the Berlin Philharmonic. All the Nazi bigwigs, of course, would attend. Furtwängler went straight back to Berta Geissmar's mother's home where, as was usual when he came to Mannheim, he was staying, and it was assumed that he had just gone there to change before the banquet. Berta Geissmar tells how he arrived, white as a sheet, and changed into ordinary sports clothes. The telephone rang again and again with enquiries about his whereabouts, but he refused to answer. At last it was too much for him. He took the receiver and screamed: 'Of course I am not coming to the banquet! And I shall never conduct the Mannheim Orchestra again! I have had enough!' He was true to his word and did not return to Mannheim until after the war.

When he left Mannheim Furtwängler considered the matter closed, but that was not to be. It must not be forgotten that even then, a mere two or three months after the Third *Reich* had come into being, all officials, whether state or municipal, had been replaced by Nazis. Furtwängler's attitude and behaviour in Mannheim was immediately reported to Berlin and to all the German towns in which he and his orchestra were to perform. He was described as 'a friend of the Jews', 'politically unsound', 'un-German' and all the rest of the customary jargon. Consequently the civic officials of the various towns they visited did not attend the concerts. The Jewish music-lovers also stayed away because they were intimidated, even though at that time they were not yet officially banned from attending public concerts or the theatre, and certain sections of the population were frightened at the thought of being seen at a concert given by an orchestra which had not yet been 'aryanised'. Furtwängler and his Berlin Philharmonic therefore had to play for the first time to halls which were half empty. Shortly afterwards they went on their usual spring tour to France, Holland and Belgium, and here again they met with a hostile reception. It is one of those ironies of fate that in Germany Furtwängler was risking his neck fighting against the Nazis for the preservation of German art and for the livelihood and safety of all those who were officially classed as 'undesirable elements', while abroad he was attacked as a Nazi supporter. In Paris things still went relatively well. It was announced that through Furtwängler's mediation, the Berlin Philharmonic had been allowed to retain its Jewish members, and the factions who had intended to disrupt the concert could be persuaded to restrict themselves to a silent expression of their opposition by showering leaflets from the balconies of the *Opéra*. But elsewhere they fared worse. In The Hague the concert was boycotted completely. In Brussels the police feared open violence and for security reasons forbade Furtwängler and his musicians to leave the hall between the afternoon rehearsal and the concert. In Antwerp it was not much different: after the concert Furtwängler had to be smuggled out of the hall through a back door and taken to the train under police escort. In those early days of the Nazi regime the free world still took a stance of determined opposition. Unfortunately, as time went on, this free world grew accustomed to the terrible things that were happening daily in Germany and became apathetic. The effective opposition which would have strengthened the backbone of the anti-Nazi section of the German population began to dwindle.

In Germany itself Goebbels, with his dual powers over the media and over theatres and musical institutions, soon managed to sweep aside mercilessly all those who in his eyes were 'undesirable' – and these were not restricted to Jews but included all left-wing elements. Only the Berlin Philharmonic was left in peace because 'Furtwängler had to be humoured'. But there was another fly in the ointment. From the outset Göring had asked Hitler if he could be put in charge of the Berlin State

5. The Nazis: 1933–1939

Opera. His wish was granted. This meant, of course, that there was one opera house, of the greatest prestige, in whose running Goebbels had no say, a fact which annoyed him greatly and led to endless squabbles. In the summer of 1933 Göring appointed Furtwängler Director of the Berlin State Opera, where Tietjen was *Intendant*, although in fact the contract with Furtwängler had already been discussed and drawn up long before the Nazis came to power. Göring of course was a Nazi like all the others, but for some reason he did not go along with the extreme anti-semitism which was the official policy, and it is well known that he once uttered the famous words: *'Wer Jude ist, bestimme ich!'* ('It is for *me* to decide who is Jewish!') To the fanatical anti-semite Goebbels such an attitude was like a red rag to a bull. There never had been much love lost between them, and they came to a bitter clash over the Berlin State Opera. Göring was generally the loser in such encounters, for his dullish intellect was no foil for the razor-edged brain of Goebbels; but in State Opera questions he could hold his own, as he had been granted all-embracing powers by Hitler himself. This was to stand Furtwängler and Tietjen in good stead in the time to come.

Meanwhile Furtwängler went his way regardless of consequences and voiced his opinions quite unconcernedly in public places where he could be overheard and denounced. There was a particular case in point – but let us hear how Furtwängler himself told it:

> On one occasion I was talking about a certain official of the Ministry of Propaganda who was a very mediocre musician, but he liked to be invited everywhere to conduct the most important orchestras. An orchestra which would not engage him could have to face all sorts of chicanery. I referred to this as 'corruption', and that must have been reported to Goebbels. He asked me to come and see him, and when I used the word 'corruption' again he lost his temper completely and raved and ranted so that he could be heard in the street. If I understood him rightly he shouted that there was no corruption in his Ministry. I answered: 'That's what we used to call it up to now!'

In July 1933 Furtwängler was appointed *Staatsrat* (State Councillor) by Göring. The title as such had already existed in the days of the Monarchy and also during the years of the Weimar Republic, but now it had a completely different meaning. Furtwängler himself was not quite sure what it

59

implied – nor were most people. In fact a 'State Council' had been formed by the government consisting of Ministers, State Secretaries and sundry functionaries, as well as nearly fifty leading figures from the worlds of art and science, and its purpose was to act in a purely advisory capacity. The inauguration of this State Council took place on 15 September 1933 with all the outward pomp and ostentation so beloved of the Nazis, and on the following day it went into session for the first time. Furtwängler was present on both occasions, after which he promised himself that he would never attend again. The whole matter would be relatively unimportant were it not for the fact that, in the eyes of people both inside and outside Germany, Furtwängler's very acceptance of the title (of which he never made use) seemed proof that he had thrown in his lot with the Nazis, and it was precisely *this* title which was later to become one of the weightiest factors for the prosecution in his denazification.

Furtwängler's second meeting with Hitler took place in August 1933 on the Obersalzberg. He arrived with a whole sheaf of memoranda and documents, as he genuinely thought that Hitler wished to discuss musical matters and would allow him to propound and explain his various concerns. But nothing of the sort happened. Hitler held forth at length, especially on the need for his anti-semitic policies, and Furtwängler could hardly get a word in edgeways. He left Berchtesgaden in a state of depression. For the first time he had come to realise that all Hitler's talk of music and artistic values was nothing but empty words: all he was interested in was politics. From Munich Furtwängler rang up Berta Geissmar and told her quite openly that Hitler was an enemy not only of the Jews, but also in general of everything spiritual. He said quite bluntly that Hitler was a narrow-minded ignoramus, and that he knew now that National Socialism was entirely hollow. Needless to say, this telephone conversation was intercepted and taken note of by the Gestapo.

Later that year Goebbels created the so-called *Reichsmusikkammer*, presided over by Richard Strauss. Furtwängler, who had been given the title of 'First State *Kapellmeister*' in June, became Vice-President of this organisation, which was designed to regulate all matters pertaining to music in Germany. After the war Curt Riess (p.156) asked him why he had accepted the post:

5. The Nazis: 1933–1939

He shrugged his shoulders. 'I became Vice-President of the *Reichsmusik-kammer* because I hoped in those days that on an official basis, so to speak, I could achieve more than I ever would have been able to achieve as a private person. At that time many people in Germany believed that the Nazis would only be able to establish themselves totally when all decent persons had shirked their responsibility.'

It is known that Furtwängler in this *Reichsmusikkammer* valiantly opposed all measures incompatible with his moral principles, but it was all to no avail. With hindsight it is easy to see that in the circumstances it was impossible for him to achieve anything.

*

Having devoted so much space to political matters we must now return to Furtwängler the conductor, and it is a continual source of amazement to me that, on the evidence of people who heard his concerts in those days, he could shake off all these adversities and aggravations the moment he stood on the rostrum. In all reports we have of him we read that he often looked tired and drawn, not surprisingly, but the moment he started conducting he was his former self. But then for him music was a spiritual force which came to him from above, and as soon as he began to make music he was submerged, enveloped and strengthened by the very sound which he himself created. It was to remain so with him always.

In 1933, as in 1934, his main task was his work with the Berlin Philharmonic, both in Berlin itself and on tours in Germany and abroad. From the autumn of 1933 onwards the Berlin State Opera was added to this portfolio and of course he also had his obligations as a guest conductor. One of his main excursions abroad was to Vienna, where in May 1933 he conducted concerts at the Brahms Centenary Festival. Furtwängler was the Chairman of the German Brahms Society, and the programmes had been agreed with the Vienna Festival Committee. In those days Vienna was still a free city, and they could do there as they liked; so in his concerts he could have Huberman, Casals and Schnabel as his soloists – a choice that hardly pleased the high-ups in Berlin. He opened the Festival by

61

delivering the Brahms Oration. Shortly afterwards, in June, he was in Paris and conducted *Tristan* and *Die Walküre*. It must have been a wonderful feeling for him to be away from the harassment and stifling atmosphere of Germany, and to be able just to make music, while meeting old friends again.

At about this time Furtwängler had to plan ahead for the forthcoming season of the Berlin Philharmonic Concerts. Again he tried to act decisively and, when discreet enquiries at the Ministry of Propaganda elicited half-hearted support, he wrote long personal letters of invitation to a number of Jewish artists, among them Huberman, Kreisler, Menuhin, Piatigorsky (his former principal cellist), Schnabel, as well as Casals who was well-known as an anti-Fascist. In these letters he propounded his belief once more that music had no concern with politics and that a beginning must be made to break down the wall that separated them. He thought that once soloists of such calibre had appeared under his baton in Berlin, other German towns would take courage and follow suit, little realising that he stood right in the midst of things, whereas all these artists were living abroad and could view matters objectively from a distance. As was to be expected, refusals soon came pouring in. The first was a cable from Menuhin and, as he was then only a boy of seventeen, his father followed this up with a letter of explanation. All the others also declined, but most of them expressed their admiration for his attempt. They just found it impossible to reconcile an appearance in Germany with their personal and artistic integrity. They did not wish to add to the prestige of the Hitler regime with a sort of *laissez-passer* which their international standing assured them, when so many ordinary people were being persecuted. The most strongly worded refusal came from Bronislaw Huberman in a personal letter to Furtwängler. The beginning is worth quoting:

Vienna, 31 August 1933

Dear Friend!

First of all let me express my admiration for the fearlessness, the singularity of purpose, the feeling of responsibility and the tenacity with which you pursue the campaign which you had started in April in order to salvage the musical life from the threatened destruction by the racial purifiers. When I place your action – the only one in present-day

Germany which has had a positive result – side by side with the deeds of Toscanini (cancellation of Bayreuth), Paderewski (Paris concert in aid of refugees) and the brothers Busch, then I am filled with a feeling of pride that I, too, can call myself a musician.

But it is just these models of a high sense of duty which must prevent me and all colleagues from making any compromises which might endanger our goal.

He proceeded to castigate the Nazis and their actions, at the same time attacking the German intellectuals and supposed anti-Nazis for not showing more strength and courage in their opposition to Hitler. He concluded by expressing his grief at exile from the Germany he loved and separation from his German friends. His last words were:

Nothing could make me happier than to perceive a drastic swing of policy – also outside the world of music – which would free my spirit from the shackles of my conscience which force me to stay away from Germany.

The letter was published widely in the free press. In the years to come he continued to make himself heard in the same vein.

Furtwängler must have been dispirited when he received all these refusals, but he did not give up the fight. He could record only one concrete success: in October 1933 the orchestra was officially taken over by the *Reich*, which meant that its finances were guaranteed by the government and its continual worries over money matters were at an end. The contract also contained a clause exempting the Berlin Philharmonic from the customary and general enforcement of 'aryanisation'. Furtwängler interpreted this clause in a broad sense, and in the Philharmonic Concerts of 11/12 February 1934 he dared play the Overture, Notturno and Scherzo from Mendelssohn's *Midsummer Night's Dream*. At Goebbels's behest there were no demonstrations or disturbances of any kind. Furtwängler probably did not realise that this apparent acquiescence was just to keep him quiet; he may have believed that it indicated a change of attitude on the part of Goebbels and that he was beginning to see things in a more sensible light. But that this was not the case Furtwängler was to discover only too soon.

The 1933/34 season was filled with musical activity for Furtwängler. There was his work with the Berlin Philharmonic as well as his duties at the Berlin State Opera where, among other operas, he conducted the first performance in Berlin of Strauss's *Arabella* and the world première of Pfitzner's *Das Herz*. Then, in January 1934, he went on tour with the Berlin Philharmonic to England and later, in the spring, to France, as had become the regular custom. On this occasion, however, and at the special request of the Italian government, a tour of Italy was tacked on after the concerts in Paris. They gave two concerts in Rome, and on the free day in between Furtwängler was received in audience by Mussolini. Not much is known about that meeting except that Mussolini asked Furtwängler his opinion of Hitler and that Furtwängler seemed to be impressed by the *Duce*. In those days the two Fascist leaders still viewed each other with disfavour, and the world at large looked upon Mussolini with a kindlier eye than it did on Hitler.

When the news of Furtwängler's interview with Mussolini reached Berlin both the Ministry of Propaganda and the Foreign Ministry were highly perturbed, for the meeting had been arranged, not through the official channels, but directly via the Italian Ambassador in Berlin – through Berta Geissmar, which made matters worse. Goebbels was enraged, but his fury knew no bounds when Furtwängler declined to conduct at the planned Nazi Party Rally which was to take place in Nürnberg in September under the slogan *Triumph des Willens* ('Triumph of the Will') even though he had apparently been asked expressly by Hitler. Furtwängler explained his refusal in the usual way by stating that he was not a member of the Nazi party and was disinclined, as a musician, to make a professional appearance at an event which was of a purely political nature. Somehow or other he managed to make this known to Hitler, who then declared that he had never expressed a wish that he should appear and fully accepted Furtwängler's explanation. Whether this was the truth or not we shall never know, but apparently even Hitler realised that it was unwise to carry things to extremes with Furtwängler.

Furtwängler, on the other hand, did not mind carrying things to extremes himself, and on the next important occasion dealt the Nazis another slap in the face. On 2 August 1934 President Hindenburg died. In his last will he had stipulated a simple soldier's funeral, but that did not suit Hitler, who loved spectacles on a lavish scale. Hitler ignored Hindenburg's wish and turned the funeral into a grandiose affair; and on 7 August Hindenburg was laid to rest in the monument at Tannenberg. Hitler himself delivered the funeral oration, and to conclude the ceremony the *Eroica* was played. Hitler had asked for it to be conducted by Furtwängler, but Furtwängler was nowhere to be found, and the time was too short even for the efficient Gestapo to track him down. Nobody knew where he was. All sorts of rumours were rife. Probably he had just gone to earth somewhere to get away from it all.

Hindenburg was dead and buried, and with him the last vestige of democracy in Germany. Sententiously Hitler declared that, since nobody now was worthy of the title of *Reichspräsident*, he would take over affairs of state and simply retain the title '*Führer* and Chancellor'. Many people failed to realise that this was, in effect, a *coup d'état*. Taken in conjunction with the *Ermächtigungsgesetz* ('Enabling Act') of 24 March 1933 and the Röhm Putsch of 30 June 1934, it put Hitler in the saddle as an absolute dictator.

By this time it was well known that Furtwängler did not go along with the Nazis, and that he helped those who were in difficulties wherever and whenever he could. It is hardly surprising therefore that, in addition to all his other tasks and duties, he had to cope with an endless stream of troubled persons. Later he said the following about this period to Curt Riess (p.174):

> Eighty per cent of my nerves and energy were spent in trying to avert injustice and in fighting the clever manoeuvres of the Nazis. It was like this: the longer the Thousand Year *Reich* lasted, the more indignant many people became about the things they saw happening, but the fewer they were who dared voice their objections. The only one whom everybody expected to open his mouth was I. And I *did* open my mouth, even though I found that it became more and more difficult for me to get a hearing in the places that mattered.

*

There were many incidents, some of a pettifogging kind, in which Furtwängler dug in his heels. A case in point was when, in Königsberg, they tried to forbid a performance of the St

Matthew Passion because of its 'Jewish' text. Furtwängler lost no time in telling Goebbels what he thought of such a ruling. Matters came to a head with the Hindemith affair. Paul Hindemith was born in 1895, studied music in Frankfurt, and in the course of time became a true all-round musician: he was not only a fine composer, but a first-class viola player proficient enough to give the first performance of Walton's Viola Concerto in 1929, an excellent pianist, a great teacher and writer on music, and a good conductor. It should also be noted that he was, in Nazi terminology, of entirely German ancestry and a pure 'Aryan'. But he was the founder of the Amar-Hindemith Quartet which contained Jewish members, and he committed the indiscretion of replying to a journalist from the Nazi daily *Der Völkische Beobachter* who had asked his opinion about the Jewish problem: 'I wish I had your worries!' – which hardly endeared him to the Nazis.

But the root of the trouble lay elsewhere. When the First World War ended Hindemith was a young man of 23. The war was lost for Germany; the old way of life had vanished forever; there was the depression and the inflation; and everywhere, particularly in the arts, was the fascination of a complete change. This applied especially to Berlin, which Hindemith had made his home. The 1920s must have been days of a glorious madness. In the visual arts movements such as cubism and dadaism were the order of the day. Similar trends existed in the world of music, and the young Hindemith felt the inner urge to belong to the *avant-garde*. He wrote chamber music incorporating saxophone, trumpet and percussion, he made use of jazz forms and rhythms, and in 1919/20 he wrote two one-act operas: *Mörder, Hoffnung der Frauen* ('Murder, Hope of Women') and *Das Nusch-Nuschi*. These, in present-day parlance, 'took the mickey' out of conventional opera. In *Das Nusch-Nuschi* an oriental potentate has his wife's lover castrated, whereupon the trombone plays a quotation from *Tristan und Isolde*: '*Mir dies, Tristan, mir!*' ('This blow, Tristan, to me!') At the première there was pandemonium. Then, in 1928/29, he composed an opera in three parts, *Neues vom Tage* ('News of the Day'), which Klemperer first performed in the Berlin *Kroll Oper* in 1929. The clattering of typewriters is heard in the orchestra, one aria is in the form of a business letter, and there is a scene in which the heroine in a bathtub sings the praises of an electric hot-water system. Unfortunately Hitler was present at a performance – Hitler with his reactionary attitude to all forms of art, to whom the ideal opera consisted of Nordic gods galumphing about the stage and blue-eyed, fair-haired heroes slaying dragons. Needless to say he was shocked to the core, and from then on the name Hindemith was a dirty word to him. When he came to power he decreed that Hindemith's compositions were 'degenerate music' – a term later taken up by Goebbels, who even organised an exhibition in Munich in 1936 under the title *Entartete Kunst*.

Naturally Hindemith outgrew this youthful *Sturm und Drang* and matured into the great artist we know him as today. In 1933 he began composing what is undoubtedly his greatest opera, *Mathis der Maler* ('Matthias the Painter'), for which he wrote the libretto himself. The story concerns the painter Mathias Grünewald (c. 1465-1528), who was in the employ of the Archbishop of Mainz. In those days an archbishop was also a worldly and political prince. It was the time of the Peasants' Revolt, and Grünewald found himself in an inner conflict: his sentiments were on the side of the peasants, but the artist within him realised that it was the Archbishop who provided his livelihood and enabled him to paint. It is another case of an artist choosing a situation from the distant past to highlight topical events, and of course the conflict between art and politics in Grünewald's day was analogous with the happenings in Germany in 1933/34. The opera therefore had a distinctly anti-Nazi flavour. Furtwängler never took in that aspect, just as he was totally ignorant of Hitler's bias against Hindemith, and he accepted the work for performance at the Berlin State Opera. He was surprised when Göring told him that it would be impossible to stage *Mathis der Maler* without first obtaining Hitler's permission but, as ever, he thought he would find a way round the problem. Meanwhile, though the score was not yet finished, Hindemith had already extracted three orchestral interludes from the opera and moulded them into a Symphony. Furtwängler gave the world première of this Symphony, *Mathis der Maler*, on 11 March 1934, intending it as a sort of preview of the first performance of the opera which, as he was fully convinced, he would conduct at the State Opera the following season. The première was received with tremendous acclaim. Even then Furtwängler did not realise that this enthusiastic applause was not only for the work, for the music itself, but in part also a political demonstration. In the months that followed the whole situation of Hindemith and his music became more and more aggravated. For Furtwängler it was a fight not so much for *one* composer or *one* opera, as for the principle of whether the body politic had a right to interfere in matters of a purely artistic nature. The crisis was reached when, for the third and last time, he made use of the public media. He wrote an article entitled *Der Fall Hindemith* ('The Hindemith Case') which he asked the *Deutsche Allgemeine Zeitung*, then the most liberal of the German papers, to publish. The Editor in Chief contacted Furtwängler to make quite sure that he was aware of the enormous risk he was taking, but Furtwängler gave him the go-ahead and the article appeared on 25 November 1934. It was a veritable bombshell: the news vendors could hardly cope with the onrush of people clamouring for the paper, and the whole edition had to be reprinted immediately. When the text of the article was published in the international press, it also created a furore.

The article is too long to be reproduced in full here. it can be found in Riess (p.179 ff.) and in *Ton und Wort* (p.91 ff.). In brief, Furtwängler brushed aside the accusation of Hindemith's 'Jewish connections', especially of his having made recordings after the Nazi accession to power with two 'refugees', considering that these 'refugees' were the former leader of the Berlin Philharmonic, Szymon Goldberg, who had given up his post to devote himself to a career as a soloist, and Emanuel Feuermann, one of Europe's leading cellists. In any case the contract had been signed much earlier. He then deals with the matter of Hindemith's first operas, regarding them as the indiscretions of a young composer who did not yet know in which direction he was going, until in his latest opera he showed that he had found his way and become a truly mature artist. He then discussed Hindemith's more recent instrumental works at length, especially his efforts to bring music to young people and provide a stimulus, a trend entirely in keeping with the spirit of the New Germany. Further he stressed that, apart from being of pure German stock, Hindemith's compositions of the last few years were marked by a true German spirit. Then he turned on those who tried to defame and inveigh against Hindemith and finished the article with the following paragraph:

> It is certain that no composer of the younger generation has done more for the recognition of German music in the world than Paul Hindemith. Besides, it is impossible to predict what importance Hindemith's work may one day have for the future. But then, that is not the question which is up for debate. Far more than the specific case of Hindemith it is a general principle which we are dealing with. And furthermore, and about that we must be utterly clear: in view of the terrible and universal dearth of truly productive musicians, we simply cannot afford to do without a man such as Hindemith.

Living in a world of his own, Furtwängler had regarded his article as one written by an artist on a purely artistic question. But everybody who read it could discern its political connotations. By coincidence (or *was* it coincidence?) 25 November 1934 was a Sunday and one of the rare occasions on which Furtwängler conducted twice on one day: in the afternoon the public final rehearsal with the Berlin Philharmonic, and in the evening a performance of *Tristan* at the State Opera. On each occasion Furtwängler was greeted with thunderous applause and everyone, especially Göring who was attending the performance at the Opera, could sense that it was not just an ovation for Furtwängler but also an anti-Nazi demonstration. That night Göring rang Hitler and told him what had happened, and Hitler imposed a ban on *Mathis der Maler*. Furtwängler's valiant efforts on behalf of Hindemith and for the freedom of musical and artistic expression had backfired completely.

In the days that followed the Nazi press denounced Furtwängler in the most vicious terms. Furtwängler himself said:

> Now at last I understood. I rang Göring and told him that I knew very well that the press received its directives from official quarters and that, if this campaign against me was not stopped immediately, I would see myself compelled to resign.

Göring listened to him but would make no decision without consulting Hitler – and Hitler refused any form of compromise. Furtwängler was informed of Hitler's decision and immediately drafted his letter of resignation from all official posts. It appeared in the press on 5 December 1934. Nevertheless Furtwängler met Göring to talk things over. Göring went into one of his screaming fits and said all he had to say at such a pitch that someone (as Furtwängler later discovered) who was sitting in the ante-room could hear every one of Göring's words and take them down in shorthand. Göring told Furtwängler that the government accepted his resignation from the State Opera and from the Vice-Presidency of the *Reichsmusikkammer* but would ask him to stay on with the Berlin Philharmonic. Furtwängler declined: for him it was all or nothing, and he also asked to be allowed to renounce the title of *Staatsrat*. But Göring declared that a title was not a position from which one could resign and that only he, Göring, was empowered to abrogate it in cases where the holder had committed an illegal or dishonourable act. It is symptomatic of those times that only one musician in Germany drew the consequences of what had by now become the 'Furtwängler Affair': Erich Kleiber resigned from his post at the Berlin State Opera, and emigrated shortly afterwards.

The Nazis immediately attacked Furtwängler from every angle. Rosenberg, the leading Nazi 'Ideologist', sharpened his poisonous pen. Goebbels roundly denounced him with every weapon of invective at his command in a big speech on 6 December 1934 to mark the first anniversary of the formation of the *Reichsmusikkammer*. He did not mention Furtwängler by name, but everyone knew whom he was attacking. None of this upset Furtwängler unduly, and he began formulating plans for his future. He had the idea of basing his conducting work on Austria and America, but first he wanted a spell of relaxation after all the nervous strain to which he had been subjected. His English friend, the author John Knittel, who lived in Egypt, had often invited him to visit. As he was now free from commitments in Berlin and had no other engagements to fulfil before April 1935, he wrote to him and invited himself for a holiday. He planned to leave Berlin for Cairo on 24 December 1934, but it did not happen.

It had been arranged long in advance that the Berlin Philharmonic would go on tour to England with Furtwängler in January 1935, and the orchestra pleaded with him to come with them, but Furtwängler was adamant. The whole affair had had far greater repercussions abroad than Goebbels had anticipated, and he wanted these concerts in England to take place at all costs so as not to lose prestige. He went to the lengths of asking Sir Thomas Beecham to take over as conductor. It is interesting that the matter was not so easily forgotten by the British. When, in May 1937, the *Sunday Times* music critic reviewed Furtwängler's performance of *Die Walküre* at Covent Garden, he added the following, referring to the events of 1935:

> The Berlin Philharmonic Orchestra with its distinguished conductor had been booked for a series of concerts in this country. The German Government, however, refused to give Herr Furtwängler his passport, and entered into negotiations with Britain's foremost conductor to take the orchestra on tour. The fee was eminently satisfactory and the artistic temptation great, but to the honour of the Englishman he refused to blackleg. Other attempts were made, but also failed. Eventually the tour was cancelled.

Late in the night of 23 December 1934, the day before he was due to leave for Egypt, Furtwängler was summoned to the presence of an important official at the Ministry of Propaganda, who told him on the telephone that he had a message for him from the *Führer*. Furtwängler went with an uneasy feeling, and he was right. Apparently Hitler had 'requested' him politely to delay his departure until the excitement had calmed down. Furtwängler knew perfectly well that a 'polite request' from Hitler was tantamount to a command and that, if he tried to defy it, all the border guards would be informed and would prevent him leaving Germany. To make doubly sure the Nazis confiscated his passport. So on the following day he left Berlin, not for Egypt but for the Bavarian mountains where he could walk through the snow and the forests and go skiing – in other words, get the physical exercise which for him was an antidote to all the worry and stress that had lately dominated him.

For the first time in years he could seriously turn to composition, and he began to make sketches for a violin sonata and a piano concerto, which were to come to fruition later. But somehow his unrest made concentration impossible, and he who loved the mountain solitude could not stand it this time for long. Other thoughts kept impinging on his mind. He saw clearly that he felt himself as a German – as a German musician and composer – and that he needed his German roots to express himself musically; but he did not wish to conduct in a Germany under Nazi rule. After long and serious deliberation, he formulated a plan: he would continue to live in Germany as a composer, but conduct only outside Germany; this he would put to Goebbels. So, in February, he returned to Berlin.

The moment he arrived he rang the Ministry of Propaganda and asked for an interview with Goebbels. All the secretaries and underlings oozed with charm and said that of course that would be possible but unfortunately the *Herr Reichsminister* was terribly busy at the moment. Would he mind waiting for a few days? As soon as time could be found they would get in touch. It was the old game of 'Don't ring us – we'll ring you!' Goebbels knew every trick when it came to a war of nerves. The cat-and-mouse game had precisely the effect he intended, for Furtwängler had a number of engagements abroad in the coming months and was worried that he would not be allowed to cross the German frontier. He wrote letters to various officials and received no answers; he tried to reach them by telephone but they were always 'unavailable'. As if all this was not enough, there were others who put a strain on his nerves. Paradoxically, they were the people who were basically on his side and wished him the best. They besieged him with letters. One faction – the smaller one – urged him to emigrate. The other, larger one implored him not to foresake them. And then there was his constant anxiety about the future of *his* Berlin Philharmonic....

*

Obviously this state of affairs could not continue indefinitely, and some sort of compromise had to be reached. At the insistence of friends, Furtwängler decided that he would conduct in Germany again but would under no circumstances accept any form of official appointment. This change of attitude was reported to Goebbels, who thereupon drafted a 'declaration' for Furtwängler's signature; but Furtwängler refused to sign. In the end Goebbels had to give in and agree to receive Furtwängler to discuss the situation in private. According to Furtwängler, Goebbels first demanded an unconditional submission to Hitler's cultural policy. Furtwängler naturally refused and threatened emigration. To cut a long story short, basic agreement was reached that he would be allowed to pursue his activities as an artist as dictated by his artistic conscience but would leave politics to Hitler and his Ministers. As a gesture Furtwängler promised Goebbels that he would give a concert in Berlin on 25 April 1935 in aid of the *Winterhilfswerk* – a charity created by the Nazis for relief for the needy during winter – and to conduct in Nürnberg during the Nazi Party Rally in September. In this way, he thought he had extricated himself from the situation honourably. He raised no objections when Goebbels proposed to publish an article in the press giving the gist of their agreement. But he had not reckoned with his wily opponent, who condensed and twisted the facts in a way to suit his purposes. When the article first appeared Furtwängler was reasonably satisfied, but people both inside and outside Germany read between the lines and gained the impression that he had finally given up all resistance and capitulated to the Nazis. It took him a long time to live this down.

Now all that was needed was an official ratification by Hitler himself to ensure that Furtwängler would be allowed to travel outside Germany. Time was running short. It had become the custom for Furtwängler to conduct the annual 'Nicolai Concert' in Vienna (a concert in aid of the widows' and orphans' fund of the Vienna Philharmonic, so named after its first conductor, Otto Nicolai), and the latest possible date for his departure from Berlin was 10 April – the precise day on which, in the morning, a meeting with Hitler had been arranged. But it was also the day on which Göring was getting married. Hitler was to be best man, the whole of Berlin was in a festive uproar, and the meeting was delayed until half an hour before Furtwängler's train was due to leave. The two met only briefly. Hitler agreed that Furtwängler would no longer be required to conduct at official – i.e. political – functions and that he would no longer hold any official position, but he did not concede Furtwängler's request that Goebbels's fabricated press release should be expanded to put Furtwängler's position in a truer light. Then, through his aide, Hitler ordered the train for Vienna to be delayed until Furtwängler was safely on board.

Less than a fortnight later he was back in Berlin, and on 25 April 1935 he conducted the Berlin Philharmonic in a Beethoven programme – the first time he appeared with them since resigning the previous December. This was the special concert in aid of the *Winterhilfswerk* which he had promised Goebbels. It was to be repeated on 3 May. The scenes in the artists' room before the repeat concert must have been extraordinary. On his arrival Furtwängler was informed that Hitler and various other top Nazis were planning to attend. This was enough to put him in a bad mood, but when he was told that, with the *Führer* present, he would have to give the German Salute – as the Nazi salute was known in those days – he went into a towering rage. '*I* don't have to salute anybody! The *audience* may greet me if they so desire, and I have to acknowledge their applause!' To underline his remarks, he ripped the wooden panelling off one of the radiators. Not that it solved the situation, but it helped him to get things off his chest. The faithful attendant of the Philharmonic, one Franz Jastrau, had already taken the precaution of closing the doors of the artists' room so that Furtwängler's voice should not be heard in the hall. Jastrau, who was never quite sober, but rarely drunk, was one of those Berlin characters, comparable to the English cockney, who remained imperturbable in any crisis. When a stalemate seemed to have been reached, he found the solution: '*Doktor*, get on the platform! Baton in your right hand! Then you can't give any German salute!' Furtwängler took his advice. He went onto the rostrum baton in hand, gave the curtest of bows and went straight into the music. After the concert the performance was repeated in inverse order: he retained his baton – which was not his usual custom – and just acknowledged the acclaim of the audience by bowing. Naturally everybody realised what was implied by Furtwängler's denying Hitler the Nazi salute, and everyone present knew from then on that he had not capitulated. There was no comment on this fact from any official quarters, even though Furtwängler's refusal to obey the dictates of the day could easily have led to his arrest. Hitler did not forget the occasion, however, and got his own back. Some time later, when Furtwängler was due to conduct Beethoven's Ninth, Hitler again announced at the last minute that he would attend. Furtwängler followed the same routine with the baton, but at the end of the concert, when he merely bowed while the soloists gave the Nazi salute, Hitler 'impetuously' jumped from his seat in the front row and 'spontaneously' shook Furtwängler's hand. He had been forewarned by his previous experience. The photographers of course were there and the picture appeared in newspapers all over the world. Those who were present knew all the circumstances, but elsewhere the photo was taken as further proof of Furtwängler's obsequiousness and was noted as yet another black mark against him.

Although Furtwängler no longer had any official ties to an orchestra or an opera house and could therefore choose which engagements to accept, his life was strenuous. On 13 May 1935 – only ten days after the Berlin concerts mentioned earlier – he left for London. Here, for the first time, he appeared at the Royal Opera House, Covent Garden, conducting *Tristan* on 20 and 24 May. His performances were greatly acclaimed, though he did not have as much rehearsal time as he might have wished. From there he went to Paris to conduct *Tristan* and *Walküre* at the *Opéra* in June – in the previous year he had conducted *Tristan* and *Die Meistersinger* – and thence to Munich where he had also been engaged for *Tristan*.[4] Most of the summer he spent in Poland and the Baltic, when he completed his Violin Sonata No.1 in D minor, for which he had made sketches as far back as 1916. For Furtwängler such holidays were always happy times, since he could get down to what he considered his real life's work: composing. We find evidence of this in many of his letters, from every period, but it is clearest in a letter to his daughter Friederike of 13 October 1937:

Until today I have been working very strenuously and with great single-mindedness. Now I have finished, and the professional duties – i.e.

[4] It should be mentioned that in his famous dialogue with Goebbels earlier that year Furtwängler had declared himself willing to conduct at any opera house in Germany apart from the Berlin State Opera.

conducting – begin again. I am very depressed, and I feel as though I have to leave my spiritual home and my true self for a long time....

This must have been the predominant feeling that led him to cancel many concerts for the 1935/36 season. He pleaded ill health, but he was suffering from exhaustion and fatigue. Yet there was still a lot of conducting for him to do. First there were *Meistersinger* performances in September 1935 in Nürnberg during the Nazi Party Rally. Then there were concerts in Berlin with the Philharmonic in September, October and November, followed by the customary tour of the UK where, between 29 November and 8 December, he conducted the Berlin Philharmonic in ten concerts from Brighton to Edinburgh. Finally there were more concerts in Berlin. No wonder he wrote to Irme Schwab on 21 December 1935:

> During the last three nights I have only slept about half an hour each night, so that I was really in an emotional despair. The whole of this tour has only shown me that a sensitive mechanism like myself is so fragile, and this form of activity so unnatural.

Christmas 1935 was spent in Munich, where he had to conduct *Meistersinger* and *Tristan*, and by 10 January 1936 he was in Vienna. The next occasion which must be mentioned is a special concert with the Berlin Philharmonic in Berlin on 25 January, his fiftieth birthday. At rehearsal he greeted the orchestra as he always did with 'Good morning, gentlemen!', adding with a half-smile: 'It's funny, but I simply can't lift my right arm!' (referring, of course, to the Nazi salute). He was presented by the orchestra with a birthday present: a beautifully bound facsimile of the autograph of Beethoven's Fifth. As the work was included in the programme, he conducted from it, though of course he did not need the score. In any case Beethoven's handwriting is so bad that it can hardly be deciphered. Then a terrible thing happened. The orchestra was playing badly, and Furtwängler lost his temper and threw the heavy score on the floor, shouting: 'I'd rather you *played* it well, Gentlemen!' In fairness it must be added that he rarely lost his temper in front of the orchestra. As a rule he would just slink off and sulk in the artists' room until the leader of the orchestra came to calm him down, which was generally not too difficult.

5. The Nazis: 1933–1939

Soon after his birthday – after conducting two performances of *Walküre* in Vienna and four of the St Matthew Passion in Berlin in February – he could at long last fulfil his dream of a holiday with John Knittel in Egypt. Taking the boat from Venice on 27 February 1936, he travelled via Brindisi, Athens and Rhodes, and reached Alexandria on 5 March. He stayed with the Knittels in Cairo, and visited Luxor and Aswan. He was able to work in peace and quiet on his Piano Concerto. This had already occupied his mind since 1930, though sketches go back to 1924. He seems to have completed most of it in Egypt but, perfectionist that he was, it was revised a good deal before it was finished. But then another bombshell exploded.

In 1936 Toscanini, then in his 70th year, resigned as conductor of the New York Philharmonic Orchestra, a post he had held for almost ten years. He suggested Furtwängler as 'his only possible successor', though this was never published in the press. There had already been clandestine negotiations via Vienna, and all major points had been clarified: Furtwängler was prepared to accept provided he was also allowed to conduct in Germany, American commitments permitting; New York agreed as long as he only appeared in Germany as a guest conductor and held no official position. Furtwängler also suggested that it might be better if he came as a guest for the first half of the 1936/37 season, and a more permanent contract be ratified later. Everything seemed to be going smoothly when he set off for Egypt in February. Of course in Egypt he was cut off from events, and he was therefore a little surprised when he received telegrams from New York enquiring as to his position with regard to the Berlin State Opera. He replied by telegram: 'I am not chief of the Berlin Opera, but conduct as guest. My job is only music.' He did not know that Göring had performed another typical act of skulduggery: when he heard of the American press notices announcing Furtwängler's appointment, he flew into a violent rage and announced that Furtwängler was being reinstated as Director of the Berlin State Opera. There was not an atom of truth in this statement, but it can be imagined what effect it had in America. To make matters worse, Hitler simultaneously occupied the Rhineland in breach of the Versailles Treaty. The two announcements, taken together, caused an uproar in New York. There were violent protests, particularly among Jewish music-lovers, and the American Musicians' Union announced that they would boycott Furtwängler. He did not discover the details of the business until he returned to Berlin, but he knew that something had gone drastically wrong when he received more and more frantic telegrams from the New York Philharmonic Society. As was ever his custom, he took direct action and cabled from Luxor on 13 March 1936:

> Detest political controversies. Am no politician, but representative of German music which belongs to whole of humanity, independent of politics. Suggest postpone my guest appearance in interest of Philharmonic Society until public realises that music and politics have nothing in common.

He was not unduly disappointed himself about the course of events, as is evident from a letter he wrote to his mother from Cairo on 25 March:

> I do not regret very much that America has fallen through, for in my view it always constituted an irksome duty. Now I shall and must make the utmost efforts to find time and room for myself and my own work during the next year. This implies cancellation of all orchestral tours, cancellation of engagements abroad, and strict limitations...

Before leaving for Egypt he had signed a guest contract with the Berlin State Opera, restricting himself to ten appearances during the season, which made it easier for him to carry out his intentions. But America, after throwing away the chance of re-engaging him after his last appearance in New York in 1927, had once more to forgo the experience of hearing him conduct. It was to happen again in 1948.

*

At the end of March he was on his way back to Europe, landing in Naples on 31 March, and then, after a short break in Zürich, he returned to Berlin. There he found out what had really happened, which strengthened him in his resolve to retire for the 1936/37 season, apart from contractual engagements, and devote himself entirely to composition. But first he had to finish up the 1935/36 season. He gave two more concerts in Berlin in April and May 1936, and after the second of these he was off to Paris immediately to conduct *Meistersinger* at the *Opéra*. A letter to Irme Schwab on 16 May after one of the performances is informative in several respects:

> The evening went relatively well. Even Toscanini, who attended the performance, supposedly was very happy with it.... Now I have four days without work in front of me, but full up with social and other obligations. I shall try to make the best of it, but just now these things bore me terribly. And Paris is so beautiful since this morning!
>
> ... Today I spent an hour and a half with Toscanini. He reproached me severely for having turned down America ... but otherwise we had a very pleasant conversation. I can understand very well the impression he makes on people.

Paris more or less marked the end of his conducting work for that season, and he could begin his 'sabbatical'. It was not quite as complete a rest from conducting as he might have wished, however, for he had pledged himself to conduct *Parsifal*, the *Ring* and a new production of *Lohengrin* in Bayreuth that summer – the first time he was to appear there since his differences with Winifred Wagner in 1931. At Bayreuth he met up with his friend Sir Thomas Beecham who had come to Germany in the company of his secretary Berta Geissmar to make preparations for the London Philharmonic's forthcoming German tour in November 1936. He was happy to see his old helpmate again. Berta's case shows how the Nazis enforced or waived their own rules whichever way it suited them. Normally it would have meant death for a Jewish refugee to set foot again on German soil – but now she stood under the powerful protection of Beecham, and the Nazis bent over backwards not to give him offence, as they regarded the visit of the London Philharmonic a matter of the highest prestige. In Bayreuth Beecham and Furtwängler discussed plans for the Coronation season of 1937 which Beecham had asked Furtwängler to share with him. Furtwängler was to visit with the Berlin Philharmonic, and to conduct two cycles of the *Ring* at Covent Garden. It would be digressing too far to describe in detail Beecham's tour through Germany, but it was not without incidents as anyone who has heard of, or read of, or perhaps even experienced,

Beecham's temperament and his own peculiar sense of humour can well imagine!

After Bayreuth, Furtwängler went into retirement. He probably spent most of his time revising his Violin Sonata No.1 in D minor, perhaps also the Piano Concerto in B minor, bringing both into their final form. He may also have done some preliminary work on his second violin sonata and even his 'official' Symphony No.1 of 1941, the germ of which dates back to that *Symphonic Largo* in B minor he had conducted in his first symphony concert in Munich in 1906. Be that as it may, the fact remains that in March 1937 in Leipzig he gave the first performance of his Violin Sonata No.1, accompanying Hugo Kolberg, the leader of the Berlin Philharmonic. They repeated the work a few days later in Berlin. It was the first time since the performances of his *Te Deum* between 1910 and 1915 that Furtwängler presented himself to the public as a composer. Of course these performances of his early works in the years before and at the beginning of the war were long forgotten by the public. Nobody therefore commented on his new maturity. What struck them most was the duration and the span of the work, and the depth of feeling it expressed. The same applied to the Symphonic Concerto for Piano and Orchestra performed by Edwin Fischer in Munich in October with the Berlin Philharmonic, Furtwängler of course conducting, which they took with them subsequently on a lengthy tour of Berlin and major German cities. This too is an extended work full of power, a worthy successor to Brahms's two piano concertos, which bears comparison in the first half of the twentieth century in Germany only with the piano concertos of Max Reger and Hans Pfitzner. It created consternation, but also admiration. The critic Oscar von Pander wrote at length about it in the *Münchener Neueste Nachrichten* praising both the work itself and the high standard of Edwin Fischer's performance. The Violin Sonata No.1, incidentally, was also the first work Furtwängler allowed to appear in print; the Symphonic Concerto was not published until 1954.

Furtwängler had intended not to conduct at all during the season 1936/37, but again this vacation which he basically wanted for composing was encroached upon. By February 1937, well before the end of the season, he was back in harness. On 10 February he conducted another charity concert for the *Winterhilfe* which was repeated on 21/22 February. This was to be a year of almost unparalleled conducting activity. He had been engaged for many appearances abroad: 1937 was the year both of the Coronation of George VI in England and of the World Fair in Paris. In March he came to London again for Beethoven's Ninth with the London Philharmonic and the Philharmonic Choir. Then back to Berlin to rehearse and perform the four operas of the *Ring* at the State Opera between 10 and 15 April, to be followed by two performances of Beethoven's Ninth on 18/19 April. On 1 and 2 May he gave two concerts in London with the Berlin Philharmonic. He stayed on in London to prepare the *Ring* at Covent Garden, which was to be one of the musical highlights of the Coronation season. Between 13 May and 1 June he conducted two complete cycles, and by 19 June he was in Bayreuth, where he was in charge of *Parsifal* and the *Ring*. His experiences during the previous year had not been the happiest, as we see from a letter to Ludwig Curtius on the day of his arrival:

> I only arrived in Bayreuth an hour ago. It was impossible to avoid another summer in Bayreuth, although it makes me very melancholy. I have become disenchanted with this business, as with so many things. The rehearsals are beginning tomorrow...

In 1937 there seem to have been further difficulties with Winifred Wagner and the Bayreuth set-up, for he refused to accept any future engagements and did not appear again in Bayreuth until 1943. When the season was over he went to Salzburg to conduct Beethoven's Ninth on 27 August, his first appearance at a Salzburg Festival. It was on this occasion that the famous meeting with Toscanini took place that was to result in the final rift between the two great men.

*

To understand the matter fully, we must examine the personality of Toscanini. Arturo Toscanini (1867-1957) was a full-blooded and temperamental Italian who had begun at the age of nineteen as a cellist and drifted, one could almost say, into conducting. He was in Rio de Janeiro as first cellist with an Italian touring opera company when one day there was a crisis. The conductor quarrelled with the management and resigned, the assistant conductor proved unacceptable, and Toscanini was asked to conduct *Aida* that same evening without a rehearsal. He did so, brilliantly – and from memory! From then on his rise as a conductor was phenomenal. Throughout his life the two main centres of his activities were to be Milan and New York. It should be noted that Toscanini was almost twenty years older than Furtwängler. Unlike Furtwängler, he was a practical and politically-minded person. At first he had been by no means averse to Mussolini – in fact, according to his biographer Howard Taubman (*The Maestro*, New York 1951), he stood in Milan as a Fascist candidate in 1919. When Mussolini came to power in 1922, this early enthusiasm waned, turning eventually to disgust until it reached the point of hatred. During this period he was the all-powerful director of the *Teatro alla Scala* in Milan, and on various notable occasions refused to play the *Giovinezza*, the Fascist National Anthem. In fact his persistent refusal may with some justification be called the outward manifestation of his protest against Mussolini and Fascism, and it was the indirect cause of his resigning from the *Scala* in 1929. But the real climax was reached in 1931. He had agreed to conduct two concerts in Bologna, and again he refused to play the *Giovinezza*. As a result he was manhandled by Fascist ruffians on his arrival at the hall for the first of these concerts. He left immediately. Both concerts were cancelled, and he said he would never conduct in Italy again. He was true to his word. He did not return to the rostrum in Italy until after the war, when he conducted a concert in 1946 at the reopening of *La Scala*. After the Bologna incident the Italian government had confiscated his passport and virtually confined him to his house; but eventually the foreign press reaction became too strong, and he was allowed to leave Italy. Naturally enough he became more and more bitterly anti-Fascist – and subsequently anti-Nazi – and eventually settled in America. But there is one point which should not be overlooked: even after he became resident in New York he was still able to return to Italy on private visits and holidays until 1939. He was not therefore irrevocably cut off from his native soil as Furtwängler would have been if he had emigrated. Moreover, as has been stated often enough, Furtwängler insisted that music had nothing to do with politics, whereas Toscanini considered them to be intrinsically interrelated.

When Toscanini, who by now utterly refused to conduct in either Germany or Italy, heard that Furtwängler was to perform Beethoven's Ninth in Salzburg where Bruno Walter and himself were also to be guest conductors, he flew into a violent rage, especially as Furtwängler was to appear there immediately after his Bayreuth season. After first refusing to come at all, he went to Salzburg with an ill grace and only on condition that he would not have to meet Furtwängler. This may not sound too drastic, but Salzburg is a small place and, as they moved in the same circles, the two men inevitably did meet. There are at least three different versions of that meeting, but the details hardly matter. The upshot was that Toscanini said that Furtwängler was a Nazi because he remained in Germany and therefore had no moral right to conduct Beethoven. Furtwängler's argument, as can be imagined, was that Beethoven was for the *whole* of humanity, and that he, Furtwängler, was fighting *his* fight in *his* way *inside* Germany. Needless to say, neither would give way or see the other's point of view, and they never met again – but it is strange that Toscanini's attitude had hardened so much politically in the span of just one year since he had reproached Furtwängler in Paris for turning down the New York offer. In all fairness it must be said that the clash between Toscanini and Furtwängler was one of personality and political conviction. As musicians they maintained the greatest respect for each other. A little episode described by Riess (p.300) which took place much later, in 1948, is typical: Toscanini's personal animosity to Furtwängler for staying in Nazi Germany was still the same, but when, at some reception, he was asked whom he considered the greatest conductor on earth after himself he first tried to evade the issue and then, pressed for an answer, furiously roared 'Furtwängler!!' – and strode out of the room. This appreciation was wholly reciprocated by Furtwängler. As late as 1953 he was approached by the French critic and composer Gustave Samazeuilh suggesting an exchange of conductors between Berlin and Paris. Furtwängler

Bernburger Str. 22 PHILHARMONIE Bernburger Str. 22

Sonntag, den 31. Oktober 1937, vormittags 11½ Uhr
Montag, den 1. November 1937, abends 8 Uhr
Dienstag, den 2. November 1937, abends 8 Uhr

II. KONZERT DES
PHILHARMONISCHEN ORCHESTERS

L e i t u n g :

Wilhelm Furtwängler

S o l i s t :

Edwin Fischer

CONCERTO GROSSO für 2 Soloviolinen, Solo-
violoncello und Streichorchester, D-dur . . *G. F. Händel*
Introduction — Allegro — Presto — Largo
Menuetto — Allegro
Solovioline: Hugo Kolberg
Solovioline: Siegfried Borries
Solovioloncello: Tibor de Machula

SINFONISCHES KONZERT für Klavier und
Orchester (Zum ersten Mal) . . . . *W. Furtwängler*
a) Schwer
b) Adagio solenne (Sehr langsam) —
Allegro — Allegretto
EDWIN FISCHER

P A U S E

SINFONIE Nr. 8, F-dur, op. 93 . . *L. van Beethoven*
Allegro vivace e con brio
Allegretto scherzando
Tempo di Menuetto
Allegro vivace

KONZERTFLÜGEL STEINWAY & SONS

85

October 1937 he had to conduct the first of the Philharmonic Concerts in Berlin. For the rest of the year he hardly moved out of Germany: there were the Philharmonic Concerts, there was the first performance of his Piano Concerto with Edwin Fischer in Munich and the subsequent tour through various cities of Germany, and there were his guest commitments at the Berlin State Opera where he conducted a brilliant new production of *Tannhäuser*. His relationship with the Berlin State Opera was somewhat ambiguous. As we have noted, he had agreed with Goebbels in 1935 that he was prepared to appear in any German opera house apart from Berlin, but he had been prevailed upon to come back to the State Opera for ten performances as a guest during the 1936/37 season. A similar contract was agreed on for 1937/38. He was unhappy about this arrangement, for it seemed to him a half-baked affair: either he was completely in charge of the opera, or he was not in charge at all. He had already expressed these worries to Göring – who, as will be remembered, was in sole control of the Berlin State Opera – but did not find a sympathetic ear. Now when Furtwängler had resigned from the State Opera in December 1934, Göring had found a replacement in Clemens Krauss. Krauss, however, did not go down well either with the personnel at the opera or with the Berlin public, and after two seasons resigned from his Berlin contract to go to the Munich Opera, where he took up a similar position in autumn 1937. After Furtwängler had conducted the brilliant *Tannhäuser* performance, Göring summoned him in November to persuade him to take over the State Opera completely again as chief conductor and musical director; but Furtwängler declined. In fact, after conducting *Tannhäuser* five times during the autumn of 1937, he asked Göring to release him from his guest contract and from the five further operatic performances he was due to conduct that season. Having mentioned the matter verbally, he wrote to Göring from Vienna on 11 December 1937, repeating his request. Göring's reply of 16 December began as follows:

Dear Mr Furtwängler!

I have received your letter from Vienna. I suppose it was just about time that I was presented with new difficulties from your side, for things had been running smoothly for almost three months!...

He went on to accuse Furtwängler of various other things which are basically immaterial but nevertheless typical of Göring. He refused to release him from the rest of his contract, and Furtwängler gave in with as good a grace as he could muster. It goes against the grain to say anything in Göring's favour; yet it must be admitted that he had some justification for his annoyance. On the one hand Furtwängler did not just want to appear at the State Opera as a guest but was prepared to sign a contract as a guest conductor; on the other, he wanted to be in complete authority yet refused Göring's offer which would have given him that authority – so what was anyone, Göring included, to do?

And then came 1938. The first few weeks were relatively tranquil, and in January Furtwängler went on his customary tour with the Berlin Philharmonic to give three concerts in England. Little did the orchestra realise that it would be their last visit to England for more than ten years. On 12 February 1938, the historic meeting took place between Hitler and the Austrian Chancellor Schuschnigg in Hitler's mountain retreat, the Obersalzberg near Berchtesgaden, which virtually sealed the fate of democratic Austria. When in early March Furtwängler was in a free Vienna for the last time, even he was aware of menacing clouds gathering overhead and noticed that the situation was getting tenser by the hour. Only a few days later, on 11 March, Hitler's armies marched into Austria. On 13 March the *Anschluss* was proclaimed, and the once free country became a satellite of Nazi Germany – now officially known as the *Ostmark*.

Once Hitler's SA and SS had established themselves in Austria, they set in motion the process of 'political co-ordination' – *Gleichschaltung*. The same racial persecution was enforced, and many persons, among them artists like Richard Tauber, Arthur Schnabel, Bruno Walter, who had escaped from Germany and believed they could build a new life in Austria had to resume their wanderings. Some found refuge in England or Switzerland, but the majority opted for the United States. In those years 1938/39 we can almost speak of a mass migration, of

87

which in modern times we can only find an equivalent, though in different circumstances and for different reasons, in the immediate post-war years. But where Austria itself was particularly affected was that the Nazis wished to subjugate it completely. Goebbels in particular wanted to seize all its art institutions and art treasures. He was particularly keen to gain control of the Vienna Philharmonic and to acquire the unique collection of music manuscripts in the possession of the *Gesellschaft der Musikfreunde*. If he had had his way he would have degraded the great capital of music to the level of a provincial town, and for once Furtwängler saw the impending danger. A senior member of the Board of the Vienna Philharmonic (and it must be noted that it was not only an orchestra in its own right but the backbone of the Vienna State Opera) came to Berlin and asked for his help. It happened that at the time a man called Joseph Bürckel was the *Gauleiter* (District Political Leader) of Austria. Whether Bürckel had much musical knowledge or any particular interest is doubtful; but he was a sworn enemy of Goebbels and would do almost anything to thwart Goebbels's plans. Knowing this background, Furtwängler agreed to resume the musical directorship of the Vienna Philharmonic as from June 1939, and in December he even accepted an appointment as *Bevollmächtigter für das gesamte Musikwesen der Stadt Wien*, which made him a plenipotentiary for the entire musical life of Vienna. He was aware that by acting as he did he was assuming untold troubles; but he had always loved Vienna, which he regarded as his second home, and by taking this step he succeeded in ensuring the freedom of the State Opera and the Vienna Philharmonic (which had already been 'nationalised' for a brief interim period) and preserving the treasures of the *Gesellschaft der Musikfreunde*.

But the conductor's life had to continue. In the early summer of 1938 London saw and heard Furtwängler for the last time until after the war. He again conducted two cycles of the *Ring* between 18 May and 7 June and, in fact, it was the very last time that Furtwängler conducted opera at Covent Garden, just as in December 1938 he made his last appearance at the *Opéra* in Paris with two performances of *Siegfried*. During the same visit to Paris he also conducted concerts, this time not with his own Berlin Philharmonic but with the Paris Philharmonic, in which he included works by Berlioz and Debussy. It was also in Paris in December 1938 that he met Friedelind Wagner, with whom he had a long talk about the future. The daughter of Siegfried and grand-daughter of Richard, she was the only Wagner grandchild with the courage to oppose her mother and the Hitler cult that dominated Bayreuth. At the age of twenty she went ostensibly for a short trip abroad and simply did not come back. Furtwängler, whom she described at the time as 'a very unhappy man', asked her about her decision to leave Germany, and what he himself should do, to which she replied quite calmly: 'You are outside Germany now! Do it like me and just throw away your return ticket.' But that was precisely what Furtwängler found himself incapable of doing for the reasons which have been stated before, even though he dreaded going back. He went back, and the only thing he could be pleased with was that he had concluded an agreement that the Berlin Philharmonic headed by himself should give concerts in Paris again in the spring of 1939, as was their custom.

But this tour was never to take place. In September 1938 the famous Munich agreement had been concluded by Chamberlain, Daladier, Hitler and Mussolini, and the Nazis had occupied the *Sudetenland*. After the assassination of an employee of the German Embassy in Paris by a Polish Jew the Nazis had organised the so-called 'Crystal Night' on 9 November 1938 when the synagogues went up in flames and countless shops and offices belonging to Jews were smashed throughout Germany, and in March Hitler took over what remained of the state of Czechoslovakia, also annexing the Memel district bordering East Prussia which had been ceded to Lithuania after the First World War. Naturally the outcry in the free world against the Nazis increased with every new act of aggression and inhumanity, and since the terms 'German' and 'Nazi' were regarded as synonymous by people outside Germany, it is not surprising that the French cancelled the projected tour of the Berlin Philharmonic. But it must be noted that, even though German musicians were no longer welcome in France, the French government made Furtwängler a Commander of the

Legion of Honour in July 1939, as if to demonstrate quite explicitly that they did not consider him as in any way involved in Nazism. Furtwängler was presented with the medal at the French Embassy in Berlin – and Hitler personally decreed that the matter must not be made known in the media.

During the few months before the outbreak of the war Furtwängler's activities abroad were much curtailed. In April 1939 he gave two concerts in Copenhagen. He also toured Italy with the Berlin Philharmonic and the Bruno Kittel Choir, and he was invited with the Berlin Philharmonic to visit Japan, where he was to give seventeen concerts in Tokyo alone. It would have been their longest tour and the farthest they had ever travelled. He was kept more than busy, for he had not only his commitments in Berlin to fulfil but had also to devote himself to his newly-acquired tasks in Vienna. In the midst of it all he did not neglect the duties he had imposed on himself: that of helping friends and acquaintances who were in difficulties. One little story from those last pre-war years is particularly worth telling. A member of the orchestra of the Berlin State Opera, Heinrich Wollheim, had been sacked because of his (partly) Jewish background and had settled on Lake Constance. His house was near to the Swiss frontier and he made it available to people who wished to escape from Germany. When this was discovered he was sent to a concentration camp. Furtwängler remembered that Wollheim was an excellent copyist and immediately applied to the Ministry of Propaganda to let him copy music for him. In this way, though he could not effect Wollheim's release from Dachau, he at least saved his life and ensured that he could live in relatively bearable circumstances. Such were the devious ways to which Furtwängler had to resort in order to achieve his humanitarian aims![5]

[5] Among the manuscripts of Furtwängler's own compositions, most of which are in the keeping of the Zürich *Zentralbibliothek*, there are several Wollheim copies, including his Symphony No.3 dated May 1954.

high. How would Furtwängler deal with it? Quite simply: he played *God Save the Queen* and then, with the strings alone, Haydn's immortal melody in the setting that Haydn himself had used as the theme for variations in his Emperor Quartet. Furtwängler played it with a calm and moving dignity, without a trace of militarism. I am convinced that no one in that huge Albert Hall took offence.

During the war Furtwängler steadfastly refused to appear in any Nazi-occupied territory, either by himself or with any of his orchestras, to the annoyance of the Nazis. It is true that during a tour of various German cities with the Berlin Philharmonic, he made a slight detour to The Hague on 23 January 1940, but at that time Holland had not yet been invaded. He visited only neutral countries and Italy. He made his point quite clear in a letter to Goebbels, saying that 'he did not wish to arrive in the wake of tanks in countries where he had once been a welcome guest'. He made only three exceptions; twice with Copenhagen (in 1942 with the Berlin Philharmonic and in 1943 with the Vienna Philharmonic) as in both cases he and the orchestra had been invited to neutral Sweden on tour and financial exigencies demanded that concerts in Copenhagen be interpolated; and once in May 1940 when in the course of a tour of Germany and Austria he gave a concert also in Prague. For the rest of it, he restricted his foreign travels to a few countries such as Switzerland. In 1941 he also took the Berlin Philharmonic to Italy. The Nazis, of course, tried everything to get him to go further, particularly to France, and they went so far as to coerce the French conductor Charles Munch – who, incidentally, had been a leader of the *Gewandhaus* Orchestra in Furtwängler's day – to appeal to him to visit Paris. Although the letter was obviously written with some Gestapo official looking over Munch's shoulder, he managed to smuggle in the words 'in agreement with the German authorities', so that Furtwängler was forewarned and could gracefully decline. But there were others who were not so fussy: Abendroth, Böhm, Heger, Knappertsbusch, Krauss and others, who cheerfully took the Berlin Philharmonic on tours to the West and East. An amusing dispute occurred after the war. A lady swore by all that was holy that she had heard Furtwängler conduct in Lyons. After much argument back and forth someone had the bright idea of asking her what the conductor looked like. She described him as 'rather portly, with a kiss curl on his forehead'. The riddle was solved. It had been Clemens Krauss!

It must be admitted that, apart from the *Meistersinger* performance at the Nazi Party Rally in Nürnberg in 1935, Furtwängler conducted the same work again on a similar occasion in 1938, and that he conducted a concert which included Beethoven's Ninth on the eve of Hitler's birthday, on 19 April 1942, in Berlin. On both occasions the arguments with which he had been presented were fairly compelling, but that would take us too far and is really beside the point. Material facts are unalterable, but the *interpretation* of a fact is subjective and is conditioned by a personal approach and attitude. It can be argued both ways: the anti-Furtwängler faction will say that he kow-towed to the Nazis when he ought to have made his position clear by emigrating. On the other hand, seen through Furtwängler's eyes, it must be admitted that if we try to wage a one-man resistance movement against a despotic regime which knows no principles of mercy or humanity, we have to make certain concessions, albeit unwillingly, in order to survive and carry on the fight. It is a question that can never be resolved to everyone's satisfaction – not, at any rate, while human beings are human beings and have their preconceived opinions. In any case, in the following years Furtwängler always managed to obtain a medical certificate to get out of such commitments.

We have the testimony of many that during the war Furtwängler was a real power of resistance against the Third *Reich*. On many occasions, in his own outspoken way, he said things which could easily have cost him his life. For instance when he came on the rostrum in Vienna and saw some Swastika flags hanging around the hall, he calmly said: 'When these rags have been removed, we can start.' Again I ask all those readers who are younger than myself to visualise the sort of courage demanded by, and the risk involved for, anyone saying something like that publicly in those times. The author Rudolf Pechel, who belonged to that group of heroes of the 20 July 1944 and the unsuccessful attempt on Hitler's life, said to

Furtwängler in later years: 'In the circle of our resistance movement it was an accepted fact that you were the only one in the whole of our musical world who really resisted, and that you were one of us.' Similarly Graf Kaunitz, also a member of that circle and a violent opponent of Hitler, stated: 'In Furtwängler's concerts we were one big family of the resistance.' These are only words, but we have evidence, incontestable evidence, in the form of recordings. In March 1942 Furtwängler performed Beethoven's Ninth, and in June 1943 his Fifth, in the Berlin *Philharmonie*. In those days the Allied air raids had not yet reached their ultimate peak, but bombs were already falling with some regularity, and if we listen to the live recordings of these concerts we are astounded by the positive and optimistic utterance, the strength transcending all mundane circumstances, with which Furtwängler could raise the 'Ode to Joy' in the Ninth and the glorious apotheosis of victory in the C major Finale of the Fifth to such Olympian heights. They are an assertion of his indomitable spirit, of his belief in that 'other' Germany of artists and philosophers, proclaiming a vision of freedom, salvation and ultimate victory of the powers of good over the powers of evil. Those who were present at the performances must have understood the wordless message which he conveyed by the music: *In hoc signo vinces*! It is not surprising that, after a performance of *Fidelio*, he once said in the artists' room: 'I am amazed that a work as topical as this hasn't been banned by the Nazis ages ago.'

In 1941 he was helped, for some months at least, in avoiding any conducting work which had a political connotation, although in a more than tragic and unfortunate way. At the beginning of March he had snatched a short holiday skiing at St Anton in the Vorarlberg. He was an excellent skier, but the season was already somewhat advanced, the snow on the slopes had become frozen, and he suffered a severe fall. Back at the hotel the doctors diagnosed no less than seventeen lesions, bad injuries to his head but, worst of all, an injury to the nerves of his right arm. His very life was in danger and the doctors were convinced that, even if he pulled through, he would never conduct again. The following seven or eight months must have been hellish, for he hardly knew what it was like to be confined to bed and inactive. He spent his time as best he could by putting down his thoughts on paper. During that period he wrote the categorical essay on the relationship Wagner-Nietzsche that was later to become so well known. But what is most germane is that through this accident fate had offered him the chance to abandon conducting and dedicate himself entirely to composing – and he did not take it. This ambivalence in his psychology is something to which we shall have to revert later in more detail. He was back on the rostrum by the middle of October. Granted, the pains in his right arm were such that he soon had to abandon the first rehearsal, and his medical advisers suggested that he should cancel the concert, as they did not think he would last more than five minutes. Yet it all went well, though in the artists' room after the concert he was in agonies. His physical constitution as well as his mental will-power must have been extraordinary, and in the months to come he simply forced his arm to obey. The incredible power of mind over matter ...

*

Fate, however, held one great boon in reserve for Furtwängler during those war years, perhaps the greatest happiness he was ever to experience in his personal life since childhood. A certain Dr Maria Daelen, a lady doctor on the staff of one of Berlin's hospitals, had been a close friend for several years, and in May 1940 her sister, Frau Elisabeth Ackermann, *née* Albert, came to Berlin. She was the wife of a German Officer of the Reserve, by whom she had three children and was expecting a fourth. Her husband, now on active service, had been called to Berlin for a conference and when he was engaged one evening suggested that she should contact her sister to have some company. It so happened that Dr Daelen had already agreed to have dinner with Furtwängler on that date, but she invited her sister to join them. It was thus quite by chance that Furtwängler came to meet Frau Elisabeth, and on his part it seems to have been love at first sight. She admits to nothing of the sort for her part: she liked Furtwängler and was tremendously awed by him as a musician, but that is as far as it went. Then, in June 1940, three days before the capitulation of France, her husband was killed in action. Furtwängler now became more open in showing his feelings; in the summer of 1941 they spent some time together, and in late December he invited her to Vienna where, in the first week of January 1942, he was to conduct *Fidelio* and *Tristan*. As he was engaged on the morning of 1 January, he procured tickets for Elisabeth to attend the famous New Year's Day Concert of the Vienna Philharmonic, and it is most endearing to hear her tell you that at that concert she suddenly said to herself: 'My God, I've fallen in love with him!' From then on things took their inevitable course. Furtwängler obtained a divorce from Zitla, and on 26 June 1943 he could marry his Elisabeth. The engagement had to be kept secret, for anything concerning Furtwängler was news in Berlin, but from the ranks of the few close friends who did know came 'well meant' warnings that he was somewhat rash in marrying a widow who was twenty-five years younger than himself and had four children. This upset Elisabeth, but he was merely amused and said jokingly: 'I shall announce that I am marrying you precisely *because* of the children, and then we shall get some peace.'

At first Frau Elisabeth with her four children remained in Wiesbaden (where she had lived before her marriage to Furtwängler) since with the increasing intensity of the Allied air raids it would have been foolish to bring her and the four small children to Berlin. Furtwängler did everything to find a home for them all. He was particularly keen on Austria, and fortune was kind to him: an aristocratic Austrian lady, a close friend of all the Furtwänglers, had an estate in Achleiten near Linz, where she provided living quarters for Wilhelm and his family. It was an ideal solution. Not only was the house situated as far away as possible from any scenes of hostility in the 'Greater Germany' of those times, but it was also on the direct Berlin-Vienna route on which Furtwängler was 'commuting' in those days. Elisabeth and the four children could be happy and relatively safe there, though the oldest boy had to travel to Linz by train every day to attend school; and upstairs Furtwängler had a large baroque room, with a beautiful view over the surrounding country, where he could work and compose in peace and quiet. It was also a good arrangement for his private life: in Berlin the faithful 'Lenchen' held the fort at the *Fasanerie*, protecting him from unwelcome visitors; in Vienna, where anyway he lived in hotels, he could snatch the odd day in the family circle in Achleiten.

I sometimes wonder whether Furtwängler ever fully realised, or appreciated, what a gem of a woman he had married. She was everything many men dream of as a wife, though not every man finds the fulfilment of that dream: a lover, a mother, a house-wife and – dare I say it? – a nursemaid at the same time. With typical masculine pride, he hated to be mothered or mollycoddled, and Frau Elisabeth had to employ all the tact and diplomacy at her disposal not to let him notice that she gave him the loving care which he actually needed. As an example I quote a little story she told me. Furtwängler's daughter Friederike came to visit him in Achleiten and wanted to rush in to see him. Elisabeth warned her that he was composing, but she said: 'Oh, that doesn't matter – he'll be glad to see me!' She was wrong. She had the door only partly open when he roared: 'Get out!!' and she beat a hasty retreat. When Elisabeth mentioned this incident to Wilhelm later and expressed the hope that she never disturbed him like that, he replied: 'Dearest, you never bother me.' Years later she said: 'You see, I knew intuitively when he actually wanted to be disturbed, and when he did not want to be bothered!'

God granted them eleven happy years of marriage. Furtwängler looked on her four children as his own, just as Elisabeth looked on his five as hers. Their bliss was complete when their own son Andreas was born on 11 November 1944.

*

Meanwhile the war continued and became more and more atrocious, as the iron grasp of Himmler and his Gestapo tightened from day to day. As a conductor Furtwängler was restricted to Germany and Austria, with the occasional guest appearance in Italy and Switzerland, and the two tours to Scandinavia. But while he fulfilled his obligations as a musician with undiminished vigour, so his resistance to the Nazi regime increased. Hitler and Goebbels bent over backwards to please him. Indeed Hitler offered him a villa as a present, and later a reinforcement of his private air-raid shelter. Furtwängler replied to Hitler personally in both instances:

At a time when so many Germans are without any home whatsoever, I cannot accept your gift.

And on 21 May 1944:

Of course I am very grateful if, during an enemy air-raid on an endangered town like Berlin, I may use a bomb-proof shelter. But at a point of time when every German has the duty to bear a burden of the war – which I neither can nor wish to evade – it seems to me that such a large architectural undertaking just for me and my family is unjustified.

This was an argument difficult to refute; and Goebbels had a further defeat after the unsuccessful attempt on Hitler's life on 20 July 1944. He instructed his henchman Hinkel to organise the publication of a brochure entitled *Wir stehen und fallen mit Adolf Hitler* ('We stand and fall with Adolf Hitler'). Invitations were sent to all prominent artists for a contribution, if only one pithy sentence. Furtwängler was the only one who wrote a long letter, stating why as a musician he did not wish to be involved in politics. The brochure duly appeared – without a contribution from Furtwängler – and we are told that he was most upset when he found that one German actor had written: 'I believe in Adolf Hitler as I believe in ultimate victory.' It annoyed him that he had not thought of that formulation himself!

Other events shattered him during that time. When he returned from his tour of Scandinavia in November 1943 he found that a portion of the *Philharmonie* in Berlin had been destroyed, though not the main body of the building. Later, on 12 January 1944, he conducted his last concert in that hall which had been his musical and artistic home for almost twenty-two years since he had taken over from Nikisch as conductor of the Berlin Philharmonic. Eighteen days later, on the eleventh anniversary of Hitler's accession to power, this spiritual home of his was totally destroyed. From his letters and conversations we know nothing of his feelings, but if he had been able to compose at the time he might have expressed himself as Richard Strauss did when he wrote *Metamorphosen* on hearing of the destruction of the opera houses in Berlin, Dresden, Munich, and Vienna.

During that whole period friends and family members warned Furtwängler to be more cautious and not so outspoken, but he would have none of it. He did not hesitate to apply to Hitler and Goebbels over and over again to safeguard musicians who were being persecuted for racial or other reasons. He was also on relatively good terms with Baldur von Schirach, the *Gauleiter* of Vienna, and had no compunction in asking him the most pointed and embarrassing questions such as: 'Actually, what *does* happen to those Jews who are being taken away?', 'What really *is* going on in those concentration camps?', 'What do you personally think about the battle of Stalingrad?' When this sort of thing became known it hardly endeared him to the Nazi regime, but he just did not care. One man, however, he underestimated: Himmler.

Himmler, the satanic chief of the SS and Gestapo, had first crossed swords with Furtwängler in a telephone conversation in 1933, which had consisted of an acrimonious verbal interchange and had ended with both men banging down the receiver simultaneously. Furtwängler had forgotten the matter; but Himmler had not, and for the duration of the Nazi regime he kept tabs on Furtwängler, intercepting his phone calls and correspondence and generally collecting material against him. He was Furtwängler's most fervent enemy, a most vicious type and the most uncouth and uncultured personality in Hitler's uncouth and uncultured entourage. He had often supplicated the *Führer* to be allowed to send Furtwängler to a concentration camp, swearing that Furtwängler was not to be allowed to survive the regime. Nevertheless Hitler and Goebbels somehow always stood up for Furtwängler and thwarted Himmler's plans, even though from later documentation we learn that, in the Ministry of Propaganda, there was the ominous memo in the files: 'There is no Jew, filthy as he may be, for whom Furtwängler does not stretch out a helping hand.' Just in time Furtwängler got to know of the undying hatred which Himmler bore against him, and if he escaped his clutches by a hair's breadth in February 1945 it was a minor miracle.

The architect Albert Speer, born 1905, was the diametrical opposite to Himmler. He was probably Hitler's closest friend – if a man like Hitler could ever claim to have had personal friends. He was well educated, cultured, an artist and – relatively speaking – a man of integrity and a gentleman. He first heard

Furtwängler conduct in his native town of Mannheim in 1922 and remained a fervent admirer ever after. In later years he came to every Furtwängler concert he could, as well as other concerts by prominent musicians, and there was a tie of sympathy, of understanding, between them. At one of the last Philharmonic Concerts, on 11 December 1944 in Berlin, Furtwängler asked Speer to come and see him in the artists' room. (This according to Speer – according to Riess the conversation took place only in January 1945.) Let me quote Speer from his own Memoirs (*Erinnerungen*, Berlin 1969, p.466):

> ... With a disarming *naïveté* he asked me straight out whether there was still a chance of winning the war. When I told him that the end was immediately in sight, Furtwängler nodded his agreement: my answer seemed to correspond with his expectations. I considered that he was in great danger, as Bormann, Goebbels and especially Himmler had not forgotten his overt expressions and his stand on behalf of the proscribed composer Hindemith. I therefore advised Furtwängler not to come back from his imminent tour of Switzerland. He replied: 'But what is to become of my orchestra? They are my responsibility!' I promised him that in the months to come I would look after his musicians.

It is true that, in anticipation of Speer's advice, Furtwängler had already taken his wife and her youngest son to Switzerland with him when he conducted for the first time at a Lucerne Festival, and had left them to stay there in the care of friends. He himself, however, returned to Germany and continued conducting in Berlin and Vienna. In his absence Elisabeth gave birth in Zürich on 11 November 1944 to their only child, Andreas, and she was fortunate enough to convey the message to him immediately. But postal services in Germany were completely disrupted, and on 14 November Furtwängler wrote to her from Achleiten:

> Through a letter from my sister from Heidelberg I have learnt that my mother has died. The funeral has already taken place, on 9 November, and unknowingly I still sent her a telegram on 12 November to tell her of the birth of our son. The telegram from Märit which told me of her death has not yet arrived ...

Then, shortly before his last Berlin concert in January 1945, a lady who had close connections with the Himmler family came to see him secretly to tell him that he was under constant surveillance by the Gestapo. His commitments at the time were a concert in Vienna, another in Berlin and several others in Switzerland. He went to Vienna, but on the day of the concert he slipped on the icy pavement and was concussed. He managed to conduct the concert nevertheless, but the doctors advised him to rest afterwards. After the concert he went on working with his secretary, Frau Agathe Tiedemann, until a quarter past two in the morning. Then he gave her leave to return to Berlin but told her nothing of his plans – he wanted her to be perfectly clear in her own conscience that she knew nothing of his whereabouts if questioned by the Gestapo.

In the small hours of the same day he left Vienna by a variety of local trains for Dornbirn where he could stay with friends for three days until his entry visa for Switzerland became valid. There are stories that he crossed the frontier on skis by night. It would be a romantic and spectacular episode, but unfortunately it is not true: on 7 February 1945 he made his way to the border post, had his passport duly stamped, and walked to the freedom and safety in neutral Switzerland, there to be reunited with his wife – and to take his baby son into his arms.

7

Freedom Casts a Shadow: 1945–1954

Wilhelm Furtwängler had regained his freedom. He was no longer subjected to the terrorism and persecution of Himmler and the rest. He was reunited with his family, and he may have thought that his troubles were over – but that was not to be.

Switzerland is a constitutionally free and neutral country, but the Swiss are also innately stubborn. It is paradoxical. In Germany Furtwängler was persecuted as an opponent of the Hitler regime – and in Switzerland, in certain political and journalistic quarters, he was hounded as a representative of precisely that Nazi system which had just done its best to exterminate him. I have frequently quoted Curt Riess, and I ought to say something more about him. Riess was born in Germany in 1902. He is an author, publicist, and journalist. As he is of Jewish origin, he was forced to emigrate, and went to America where he acquired US citizenship. Later he settled in Switzerland, where he still lives, and worked at first as a foreign correspondent. When Furtwängler escaped to Switzerland in February 1945, he was one of his most vociferous opponents. Let me quote him from his own book (p.273):

> Amongst those who at that time were of the opinion ... that Furtwängler was not a desirable person in Switzerland, I was also one, and I thought it absurd that this 'Nazi' should be allowed to conduct concerts here.

Later he met Furtwängler, who showed him documentary evidence of which he was unaware. In the light of this he wrote the first book on Furtwängler after 1945. It is the most glowing rehabilitation conceivable: *Wilhelm Furtwängler: Musik und*

7. Freedom Casts a Shadow: 1945–1954

Politik. Furtwängler, who valued Riess highly, did not approve of the book, feeling that it did not say enough about him as a musician, as is shown by a letter to Riess on 25 September 1953, but in a sense he was wrong: Riess had written his book in precisely the context of his subtitle – *Musik und Politik*.

Furtwängler had been invited to Switzerland about eighteen months before by Ernest Ansermet to conduct two concerts with the *Orchestre de la Suisse Romande*, and it was on the basis of this invitation that Furtwängler had been given his entry visa into Switzerland. He was still allowed to conduct the two concerts in Geneva and Lausanne on 12 and 14 February 1945 respectively, but the concert with the *Tonhalleorchester* in Zürich on 20 February (which should have been repeated on 25 February) was banned by the local government. The Winterthur authorities were more daring and allowed him to conduct Bruckner VIII on 23 February, though the police and fire brigade had to be called in to scatter the demonstrators with water cannon. In the concert hall, however, all was peaceful. The concert was to be the last that Furtwängler conducted for the next two and a half years.

But let us not be prejudiced: apart from these journalistic and governmental factions there were many Swiss, mainly in artistic and cultural circles, who were disgusted by the reaction and voiced their opinions in no uncertain way in favour of Furtwängler. He probably did not know how many good friends he had there to support him. It must not be forgotten that he had not been clever enough to open a bank account abroad. All his assets were in Germany. These of course were now frozen and, once his earnings from those last concerts in Geneva, Lausanne and Winterthur were used up, he was virtually penniless. Friends came to his assistance. There was the great patron of music Dr h.c. Werner Reinhart who gave him generous financial support; also the solicitor Dr Walter Strebi, a town councillor in Lucerne, who helped him both legally and financially; and, last but not least, that great advocate of Fresh Cell Therapy, Dr Paul Niehans, who had his clinic *La Prairie* in Clarens near Montreux on Lake Geneva and gave him a roof over his head. To Furtwängler, who was intensely independent by nature, it was of course anathema to have to rely on 'alms', but he was nevertheless deeply grateful and accepted his fate.

103

It was only with difficulty, and only through the intervention of men like Ernest Ansermet and others, that the Canton Vaud was persuaded to give Furtwängler the *Permis de Séjour*, and even then it had to be renewed every month or two. Nevertheless he now had a place where he was entitled to live. He remained in Clarens for the rest of his life, and Frau Elisabeth still lives there.

These two and a half years are among the strangest in Furtwängler's life. He agreed with the Swiss authorities to make no comments – verbal, written, broadcast or otherwise – about his defence and rehabilitation. He also refused to conduct anywhere until he had been 'denazified', even though the Austrian authorities had cleared him of any Nazi involvement as early as March 1946 and had offered him Austrian nationality. During this whole period he must have been in the deepest depression, even though he once said to his wife that later they might remember it as one of the happiest periods of his life because he was free from conducting duties and could really dedicate himself to his life's ambition: composing. Indeed during these years he was able to complete his Symphony No.2 (on 18 October 1945, according to a letter he wrote to John Knittel that day) and begin his Third.

Nevertheless his ostracism hurt him deeply, and also the continual delay of his 'denazification'. One of the most poignant expressions of this man not given to voicing his personal feelings was in a letter of 19 March 1947 to his friend Boleslav Barlog, of whom more shall be said later:

> I can just see it coming: all my colleagues will again be free and reinstated in all their honours and offices, and only I, who am the only one who has really made opposition, who has really gone through torture, will probably be condemned to disbarment from Germany for years to come.

For almost two years Furtwängler fought the battle for his rehabilitation, for his honour. There is no point in going into details, for these can be read up by anyone interested in Daniel Gillis's *Furtwängler and America*, which gives a precise account. Suffice it to say that he fought his own battle honestly and valiantly. Most other nations had granted him absolution; it was only the American factions that opposed him so viciously.

He had many enthusiastic sponsors, and it is worth noting that eminent persons spoke in his favour.

Yehudi Menuhin, who had come to Europe in the wake of the victoriously advancing Allied armies, had fulfilled his promise to General de Gaulle that he would be the first to play in a liberated Paris – the Mendelssohn Violin Concerto. He went on to Amsterdam and Brussels, Prague and Vienna, and finally to Berlin where he appeared not in a concert hall, but in a former concentration camp, where many of the inmates still lived for want of a place to go. While he was in Berlin he made detailed researches to discover everything he could about Furtwängler and his moral conduct during the previous twelve years. On his return to America Menuhin stated categorically in an interview that Furtwängler had behaved decently and honourably during the Third *Reich*, and that he was being treated unjustly. A canard was then launched in the USA by the anti-Furtwängler faction, saying that he was considering a return to the USA. There was not a word of truth in it, but in a second interview Menuhin jumped to his defence again:

> As far as concerns Nazis penetrating the American scene, I think my name, my position and the ideals for which I have fought should exempt me from any accusation that I might be tempted to introduce Nazis into the United States.

Later there was a statement from Menuhin's father, Moshe. He was born in Russia of an orthodox Jewish family which had emigrated to Palestine and eventually settled in America, where he later became Professor of Hebrew at a university in California – and it should be noted that Hebrew was spoken at home and therefore became Yehudi's mother tongue. Hardly any Nazi sympathies in that household! He wrote:

> Wilhelm Furtwängler was a victim of envious and jealous rivals who had to resort to publicity, to smear, to calumny, in order to keep him out of America so it could remain their private bailiwick. He was a victim of the small fry and selfish and puny souls among concert artists, who, in order to get a bit of national publicity, joined the bandwagon of the professional idealists, the professional Jews and the hired hands who irresponsibly assaulted an innocent and humane and broad-minded man, all because by association, by birth, he was a German. We Jews are very sensitive when all of us are called names because one scoundrel of a Jew may have

105

acted immorally; yet just because the German people were captives of murderers and cannibals called Nazis, who were insane with racist nationalism, just because many of them conformed and obeyed their Führer, is there any excuse for taking an individual, decent, noble German and fouling his name, boycotting him, refusing him his rightful position in America, not once, but time after time ...

The fact that the Austrian government had declared Furtwängler blameless from any Nazi implications cut no ice with the Allied authorities, and they did not put the stamp of approval on this denazification. At about this time Curt Riess had a conversation with General John McClure of the American Information Control Division and was assured that the Furtwängler affair would be cleared up 'within a matter of four weeks or so'. But these 'four weeks' stretched into many more weeks and months. Without Furtwängler's knowledge Yehudi Menuhin sent a long telegram to General McClure, of which the most salient sentence is: 'As a military man you would know that remaining at one's post often requires greater courage than running away.'

The Russians, on the other hand, were more liberally-minded and at the same time more sly: they offered Furtwängler the post of Artistic Director of the East German State Opera. Furtwängler was loth to accept, as he wanted to return to his Berlin Philharmonic. When Riess reported this to General McClure, lo and behold, all prevarications were set aside and a date was fixed for his denazification tribunal on 12 December 1946.

At this tribunal all sorts of accusations were brought against Furtwängler, but he was able to contradict them all. Nevertheless there were insufficient witnesses on his own side, and his personal feelings can best be appreciated if one looks at a photo taken of him at this tribunal, of which I have found only one reproduction, in *Furtwängler im Urteil seiner Zeit* (ed. Martin Hürlimann, opposite p.193). It is the face of a man dejected, weary unto death – but unbowed. A second tribunal took place on 17 December 1946 where Furtwängler could present witnesses in his defence. Let me name a few. Boleslav Barlog, who had been hampered in his career in the theatre under the Nazis for so many years and then became one of the great masters of the stage after the war, testified for Furtwängler:

> For the duration of the Third *Reich* Furtwängler was one of the reasons why it was worth staying alive. Every few weeks or so a concert conducted by Furtwängler – if we could have that, then there was no need to despair utterly ... I am willing to place all the political credit I hope to possess completely into the scales in favour of Furtwängler.

Then there was Clemens Herzberg, Max Reinhardt's former business manager. (Max Reinhardt himself had died in New York in 1943.) When he appeared as a witness, Herzberg was asked by the presiding judge whether he had ever been a member of the Nazi party. Now it so happened that Herzberg, a Jew, had lived in hiding in Berlin throughout the past twelve years. He also had a nose of generous proportions. He just pointed to it and said: 'I don't think you had a proper look at my nose!' Finally there was Jastrau, the orchestra attendant of the Berlin Philharmonic, who looked at these exalted judges and said in the broadest Berlinese: *Ik muss mir ja sehr wundern, wat die da mit unserm Meester machen!* ('I must say, I am very surprised at the way they're treating our boss!')

There was a unanimous verdict of 'Not guilty'. Of course Furtwängler thought he was now in the clear, but it was not to be: things never went that smoothly for him. Again weeks passed, and on 25 January 1947 Barlog once again published a long article in *Der Kurier*, a Berlin newspaper sanctioned by the French occupation authorities, defending Furtwängler once more and accusing all those who were harassing him. Then he discovered that the reason for the delay in ratifying Furtwängler's denazification was, ostensibly, a shortage of stationery in the American Information Control Division: a complete report required 2000 sheets of paper. Barlog, with his typical sense of humour, made a public appeal. This met with a great response, and soon he was able to deliver to the Allied Control Commission a small vanload of typing paper – only to have it returned to him and be told off for 'unwarranted interference'. The object of the exercise was nevertheless achieved, and the Control Commission got a move on. Furtwängler's denazification was officially ratified on 27 April

1947. (Thus according to Gillis. The exact date varies in different sources – some put it as 2 May.)

After all he had been through, this waiting must have been torture for Furtwängler, especially as he had commitments to conduct in Rome and Florence in April. Fortunately the Italians did not concern themselves much about Allied decisions, and Furtwängler could therefore conduct again on 6 April 1947 in Rome, more than two years after his last concert in Winterthur in 1945. Frau Elisabeth tells me that he was a little apprehensive about whether he would still be able to conduct after so long a break, and he was therefore rather nervous. Once he was on the rostrum, however, the spirit of the old Furtwängler reasserted itself triumphantly. He was also booked to conduct a concert in Milan; but, as he wrote on 14 May 1947 to Fritz Zweig, a former *Kapellmeister* at the *Städtische Oper* in Berlin who had emigrated: 'This was cancelled at the last moment after a telephone protest from Toscanini. I was dismissed and Issay Dobrowen was engaged to replace me.' As Gillis writes: 'This was indeed ironic, since Dobrowen owed his escape from Nazi Germany to Furtwängler alone.' If we look back on the incident in Berlin in 1933 when Richard Strauss took over a Bruno Walter Concert, is this not a strange reversal of fate?

Now that Furtwängler was in the clear he was in demand as a guest conductor all over the world. Once again he was frustrated in his ambitions to have time free to compose. On 25 May 1947 he conducted his first concert with *his* Berlin Philharmonic, an all-Beethoven programme, which had to be repeated on 26, 27 and 29 May before enthusiastic audiences. There have been hostile comments regarding this, his first reappearance with that orchestra which was so peculiarly his own. One particularly aggressive critic was Erika Mann, the daughter of Thomas Mann who, though not Jewish, had been deprived of his German nationality and had emigrated. Mann could never forgive Furtwängler for not having done the same and his daughter followed his line. Though she had not been present at the concert, she stated in an interview in New York that the ovations were nothing but a neo-Nazi political demonstration. It was indeed a demonstration – but a demonstration for a musician, an artist, a freedom fighter whom the people of Berlin could justly claim as their own.

At first Furtwängler took up conducting again because he had to earn money to repay the debts he had contracted during his years of inactivity – this, for him, was a matter of honour. At the same time he allowed himself to be enticed anew into the world of 'conductor/managing'. There is, I believe, a Chinese saying: 'He who rides the tiger cannot dismount.' This was precisely his dilemma. In a letter to the pianist Johannes Bork from Clarens on 9 July 1951 he outlined the position concisely:

> The way the battle for survival has developed these days – even as far as conducting is concerned – there would seem to be only two alternatives: either to give up and resign, or to join the rest and go full steam ahead – as though the dual activity of composing and conducting were no longer permissible.

To return to Menuhin, though he had only known Furtwängler from his recordings and had never met him personally, he had a great admiration for him. As mentioned, he had refused an invitation to be Furtwängler's soloist at the Berlin Philharmonic concerts in 1933 for reasons of conscience. Then, after the war, he had become one of Furtwängler's staunchest supporters after thoroughly sifting the evidence. Some time early in 1946, in the Hôtel Trois Couronnes in Vevey, the Menuhins and the Furtwänglers first met over lunch. The bonds of sympathy between the two men, the bonds of musicianship, were forged, and they remained fast friends to the day of Furtwängler's death. They first made music together in Salzburg on 13 August 1947 when Furtwängler accompanied Menuhin in the Brahms Violin Concerto. Then, on 30 August 1947, Menuhin played Beethoven's Violin Concerto under Furtwängler in Lucerne, and again on 28 and 30 September and 2 October 1947 in Berlin. Karla Höcker gives part of the text of a talk in German which, much later, Menuhin gave on Berlin Radio:

> After playing the Beethoven Concerto with him for the first time I was so deeply moved that I promised myself never to play that Concerto again with any other conductor. Of course that is impossible, and I have often played it with others and with great enjoyment since that time. But I was

109

so overpowered by this precious, this unique experience that I did not want it ever to be effaced or fade away in my ears – the way in which he had conducted this Concerto.

Once Furtwängler had conducted these concerts in Rome and Florence in April 1947 and the first concerts in Berlin in May, life was more or less back to normal. It is true that he had determined to ease up on his conducting commitments and had therefore refused to sign a contract with the Berlin Philharmonic,[1] although they urged him strongly. Frau Elisabeth told me that he explained his position to many agents and orchestra managers. They all agreed whole-heartedly with him, but invariably added that of course he must spare himself – but not at the expense of *their* orchestra, *their* town, *their* organisation! Much later he said in a conversation with Riess (p.250):

> I had hoped to be able to cancel this or that concert, to make myself free for a few months, perhaps even for a whole year.... But this just does not work out. When you are caught up with this business it devours you. The only way is to take a radical step like Liszt, who stated categorically one night: 'I shall never play again.'

So Furtwängler went on, even when the financial need was no longer pressing. Nor should we forget that, in 1947, he was 61 years old – by no means old as conductors go, but no longer a youngster who could boast boundless energy.

It would be tedious to list all Furtwängler's activities during those years from April 1947 on. Suffice it to give some of the highlights. His first triumphant appearance in Berlin in May 1947 has already been mentioned. In August he conducted his first concerts in Austria, in Salzburg, with the Vienna Philharmonic Orchestra, in the second of which, in the Brahms Concerto, Menuhin was his soloist for the first time. Then, also in August, he participated in the Lucerne Festival, and in September Menuhin was his soloist in the Beethoven Concerto in Berlin. There is a story of this occasion worth relating. The *Philharmonie* being only a heap of rubble, the Berlin Philharmonic had found a home in a former cinema, the

---

[1] In fact he signed a contract with the Berlin Philharmonic only as late as December 1951 but otherwise remained free of contractual obligations and only conducted in the capacity of a freelance.

7. Freedom Casts a Shadow: 1945–1954

Titania-Palast, which also served for shows for the American occupation troops. Menuhin and Furtwängler were rehearsing the Beethoven when suddenly a door opened and a huge American Military Policeman burst in. He came up to the rostrum, patted Furtwängler genially on the back and said: 'It's time to finish.' Furtwängler was struck dumb, but Menuhin stepped up to the policeman and hissed: 'Stop that nonsense!' He smiled and nodded to Furtwängler, raised his violin, and both men were back in the realms of Beethoven's music. After a short while the American shrugged and walked off, as much as to say: 'What can you do with such lunatics?'

In 1947 Furtwängler appeared again for the first time after the war in Berlin as an opera conductor with two performances of *Tristan und Isolde* (this time with his admired Frida Leider – not as Isolde, but as producer!). He conducted in Stockholm and in Leipzig; and in November he appeared for the first time again with the Vienna Philharmonic in Vienna. In January 1948 he conducted the *Orchestre du Conservatoire* in two concerts in Paris, including in his programme two of the *Nocturnes* of Debussy. It was the first time he had stood before a Paris audience since before the war, and as there had been minor demonstrations in various other towns in Europe the French authorities were somewhat apprehensive, for few countries had suffered so much under Nazi occupation as France. But there was no cause for concern: that innately cultured nation recognised the greatness of the artist, acknowledged his constant refusal to conduct there during the years of the war despite the urgings of the German government, and greeted him with open arms. How very different from the United States! In February/March 1948 Furtwängler returned to England for the first time and conducted the London Philharmonic in London, Birmingham, Leicester, Watford and Wimbledon in no fewer than ten concerts. Recently I was speaking to the English composer Leonard Salzedo, who was then a violinist in the LPO, and he told me that playing under Furtwängler in those concerts was the greatest experience he had had in his career as a musician. Furtwängler returned with the Rome St Cecilia orchestra for two concerts at the Edinburgh Festival in September, with the Vienna Philharmonic for five concerts in

111

London's Albert Hall in September/October, and with his own Berlin Philharmonic (concerts in London, Liverpool, Birmingham, and Oxford) in November 1948.

Furtwängler has been described as a 'travelling conductor'. This is both true and untrue. Granted, he travelled a good deal in those post-war years, but his travels were mainly restricted to Western Europe. Before 1939 he had only been out of Europe for those concert engagements in the USA in 1925-29 as a guest conductor (if we exclude the holiday with John Knittel in Egypt in 1936, which was purely private). After the war he went twice as a guest conductor to Buenos Aires (in 1948 and 1950) and for one concert to Caracas (in March 1954). The only time he went out of Europe with an orchestra of his own, the Berlin Philharmonic, was in April 1951 to Cairo and Alexandria.

I will not bore the reader with a long list of his commitments and obligations, but will give a brief summary of his activities in the calender year 1949 – a year I have picked at random. In that year he conducted 75 public concerts and eight opera performances in 34 towns, and in addition worked in the studio (radio and/or gramophone recordings) for fourteen days. He also gave several lectures. Nor must we forget that, though many of his concerts on tour were repeats, he had already spent a great deal of time beforehand re-learning the scores and many days in preliminary rehearsals. Truly a tremendous workload for a man who was by now 63.

*

Let us return to the relationship between Furtwängler and America; and here it is important to state that the constant animosity of the US dates back to his second and third visits as a guest conductor to America in 1926 and 1927, six or seven years before the advent of Hitler. It originated therefore not on political but on personal grounds, and later developed into the quite unmusical and 'musico-political' confrontation between Furtwängler and Toscanini in which, at the time, neither of the two great musicians was a direct protagonist. The whole business flared up again in 1936, for reasons we have already noted, when Toscanini proposed Furtwängler as his successor as

Musical Director of the Philharmonic-Symphony Orchestra of New York. It is true that in 1926/7 the fault lay partly in Furtwängler's ignorance of the workings of musical life in America. Furtwängler was no partygoer, disliked social life and, from his European viewpoint, paid scant attention or respect to the socialites who ruled the musical roost in America. That was his downfall.

America always spelt bad luck for Furtwängler. In 1948 the Vice-President of the Board of Directors of the Chicago Orchestral Association invited Furtwängler to become the chief conductor of the Chicago Symphony Orchestra. He debated the matter for some time, but eventually gave in and signed a contract. This created a furore: many American musicians of note were infuriated and swore they would never play in Chicago if Furtwängler were Musical Director. On the other hand some staunch friends, among them Bruno Walter, Rafael Kubelik and Heinz Unger (himself a Nazi refugee), stood on Furtwängler's side. Above all, Yehudi Menuhin supported him once again by telegraphing the Chicago Board as follows:

> I shall have to give up the pleasure of playing with the Chicago Symphony Orchestra until this affair has been clarified.... Furtwängler showed firm resistance to the Nazis; he kept as many Jews as possible in the Berlin Philharmonic Orchestra, never undertook propaganda tours, was never a member of the Nazi party ... He has been denazified by those responsible for clarifying his case, and it is not for us to question their judgment.

But the opposition was too much. In the end Chicago asked him to stand down, but Furtwängler refused: after all, he had signed a contract and was legally entitled to stand by its terms. In the end there was a compromise: Furtwängler allowed Chicago to annul the contract, feeling that a withdrawal would be a silent acknowledgment of his guilt, but he forbore from exacting his fees, though at the time he could well have done with the money he was due.

About three years later, in August 1951, a somewhat similar event occurred. Rudolf Bing heard Furtwängler in Salzburg in performances of Mozart's *Zauberflöte* and Verdi's *Otello*. Bing, born in Vienna in 1902, had been active in opera in Germany and Austria until Carl Ebert brought him to England in 1934.

113

He was General Manager of Glyndebourne from 1936 to 1946 and became a naturalised British subject. He was a co-founder of the Edinburgh Festival, of which he was Director from 1947 to 1949, and finally became General Manager of the New York Metropolitan Opera. He was knighted in 1971.

Bing immediately realised Furtwängler's greatness and invited him to become the musical head of the 'Met' – a proposal with which Furtwängler sympathised. But after Bing's return to New York the same old troubles flared up, and Bing was compelled to write a contrite letter saying that he would have to renege.

So the anti-Furtwängler clique had successfully managed to deprive the American musical public of his talents: once in 1927/8, once in 1936, and again in 1948 and 1951. True, there were firm commitments for Furtwängler to come to America in January 1955 with his Berlin Philharmonic, but by then it was too late. He had died in November 1954, and this first American tour of the Berlin Philharmonic was conducted by Herbert von Karajan.

Curt Riess tells us in his book (p.304) that he only got to know the whole truth during a stay in New York much later:

> I asked: 'Actually, what was the motivation for these strange actions?' A well-known musician who begged me not to mention his name gave me the answer: 'They feared Furtwängler. Everybody knew that, once he had conducted in America again, he would get all the best offers. The other conductors said to themselves that they would have everything to lose if he were to come ...' And nothing has changed since then.

This was written in 1953.

*

Little more need be said about the few remaining years of Furtwängler's life. In Berlin he retained his *pied-à-terre* at the *Fasanerie* until the division between East and West Berlin became stricter and the crossing point at the Glienicke Bridge was closed. As this would have meant an enormous detour when driving to the Western Sector, he gave up his home in Potsdam, where he had lived since 1932, and took a small flat in the West Berlin suburb of Dahlem (Meisenstrasse 1a). Of course the faithful Lenchen came with him. In Switzerland he also had good luck. On one of his walks he met the shipping magnate Rickmers, a man of enormous wealth who owned a large villa in Clarens, the *Villa l'Empereur*. As Rickmers was getting on in years he only occupied a smaller house at the edge of his park. He offered Furtwängler the use of his large music room, and somewhat later, in 1947, Furtwängler was able to rent the entire villa, which gave him and his family a real home again. Then, in May 1954, his finances were such that he could consider buying a house of his own in Clarens, the *Villa Basset-Coulon*. Apart from the holiday chalet near St Moritz it was the only house he ever owned, but fate granted him only a few months to enjoy this happiness.

On the professional front life fell into the old routine: conducting, conducting, conducting, sometimes with his own orchestras – the Berlin and Vienna Philharmonics – sometimes as a guest conductor with the orchestras of various cities. His three tours to South America (in 1948 and 1950 to Buenos Aires, where he conducted the *Orquesta del Teatro Colon* and the *Orquesta Sinfonica de Buenos-Aires*, and in March 1954 to Caracas, where he gave two concerts with the Venezuelan Symphony Orchestra), and his tour in April 1951 to Cairo and Alexandria with the Berlin Philharmonic have already been mentioned. For the English reader it may be of particular interest that, after those concerts in 1948 which have been cited, he returned to Britain in 1949 with the Vienna Philharmonic. More important is the lasting relationship with Walter Legge's Philharmonia Orchestra that began in May 1950: from 1950 on he conducted this orchestra, with which he also made many gramophone recordings, only in London (and subsequently also in Switzerland), apart from one concert in London on 22 April 1953 with the Berlin Philharmonic and, on another visit, four concerts at the Edinburgh Festival of 1953 with the Vienna Philharmonic. He was last heard in the flesh in an all-Beethoven programme at the Royal Festival Hall on 12 March 1954, again conducting the Philharmonia Orchestra.

He was in demand all over Western Europe: Italy, Switzerland, France, the Scandinavian countries and the Netherlands. He was a regular guest at the Lucerne and

Salzburg Festivals, and it is notable that he turned markedly towards opera, especially Wagner's *Ring* of which he conducted no less than three complete cycles at the *Teatro alla Scala* in Milan in 1950 as well as another cycle for *Radio Italiana* in October/November 1953. Two things are also worth noting. One is that, apart from conducting Beethoven's Ninth twice in Bayreuth, he never appeared there again as a Wagner conductor. The other is that, although he was so fervently devoted to Bruckner's Symphony No.9 which he had conducted in 1906 in his very first symphony concert in Munich, he never played this work again after 1947.

In 1952 during rehearsals in Salzburg for the first time in his life (apart from accidents) he was struck down by illness. It was a serious case of pneumonia and the doctors even suspected meningitis. He had to go to hospitals and sanatoria, and he was out of action for about five months. He was confident that he would quickly recover, but unfortunately they gave him vast doses of antibiotics. Now, as every musician knows and few doctors will admit, antibiotics have an unfortunate side-effect: they affect the hearing. He recovered, but in January 1953, while conducting Beethoven's Ninth in Vienna, he fainted during the third movement. Few details are known, but the fact remains that against his wishes they gave him antibiotics again. From then on his hearing deteriorated. Not many people knew about it, but the knowledge perturbed him greatly. He consulted doctors and psychiatrists, and even considered wearing a hearing aid, but was advised against it. Naturally the symptoms were aggravated by psychological stress and were especially evident when he was conducting his own compositions – something which always frightened him, as he felt he was baring his innermost self.

It must have been a great ordeal to conduct the first performance of his Symphony No.2 in Berlin on 22 February 1948. Hindemith was present at this *première*, but clearly the music was not to his liking. A friend and pupil, who was later his successor as professor of Viola at the Berlin *Hochschule für Musik*, told me of the aftermath. Furtwängler naturally expected Hindemith to come and see him in the artists' room after the concert, and of course he came; but what did he say?

7. Freedom Casts a Shadow: 1945–1954

With innate diplomacy he placed both his hands on Furtwängler's shoulders and said: 'My dear Furtwängler, the things you
write!!' – and Furtwängler took the compliment with a beaming
smile without realising the ambiguity. (Frau Elisabeth tells me
that the story as such is true but that it occurred after a
performance of the Symphonic Concerto.)

During the ensuing years he was to conduct the Symphony
nearly twenty times in Germany, Switzerland and Austria,
coupling it most frequently with Beethoven's First in the second
half as if to accentuate his inner affinity with that giant. This
was also his programme in September 1954 in the last public
concert he conducted in Berlin. It was his greatest wish to hear
this composition performed by some other conductor, so that he
could sit in the hall and listen, but his dream was not fulfilled.
During those last days when he was in the sanatorium his friend
and younger colleague Eugen Jochum was preparing a
performance in Munich with his Bavarian Radio Orchestra.
Furtwängler hoped to be present, but it was too late.

In August and September 1954 Furtwängler again conducted
at the Salzburg, Bayreuth and Lucerne Festivals, and in
between even gave a concert at the Besançon Festival. Then,
from 28 September to 6 October 1954, he was in Vienna, where
he recorded Wagner's *Walküre* complete. It was the last time he
conducted. Incidentally, though it is often said that he did not
complete this recording and that the last side was performed by
Karajan, Frau Elisabeth – who was present at all the sessions –
assures me that there is no truth whatever in the story and that
the recording is Furtwängler's own from first to last. On the
return journey to Clarens Furtwängler felt unwell and caught a
chill. But Frau Elisabeth could not persuade him to keep to his
bed: he thought he could cure himself by long walks in the fresh
air. However, in the night from 5 to 6 November he said to her:
'From this illness I shall die, and it will be a very easy death.
Don't leave me for a minute.' But none of this prevented him
getting up the next day, going for walks and working on his
Third Symphony, which had just arrived from the copyist. In his
last diary entry he jotted down titles for the four movements:
Das Verhängnis ('Destiny'), *Im Zwang zum Leben* ('Force of
Life'), *Jenseits* ('Hereafter'), *Der Kampf geht weiter* ('Battling

On'). This is indicative of his state of mind, since it was not his habit to give his music programmatic titles. We shall come back to this point later.

His condition deteriorated. Frau Elisabeth called in his personal physician who diagnosed bronchial pneumonia, and so she drove him to the clinic Ebersteinburg near Baden-Baden on 12 November 1954. She told me herself that, although used to driving long distances, she had a cramp from gripping the steering wheel so tightly, and she relaxed again only when she saw him comfortably in his bed. But he whispered to her: 'You know, they all think I have come here to get well again. But I know I have come here to die.' From then on she stayed with him day and night except once on his last day so as not to inconvenience the doctors and nurses who were giving him a blood transfusion. His personal physician assured her that bronchial pneumonia was nothing to worry about in the current state of medical knowledge, but another authority who was called in later wrote in his memoirs, citing Furtwängler's case, that doctors had little chance of success once a patient had decided for himself that he no longer wished to live.

One thing struck Frau Elisabeth particularly. When he had been ill in 1952 he had been cheerful and confident and had continued in his usual manner, walking up and down the room, humming to himself and conducting an invisible orchestra. Now he lay perfectly calm, not moving at all, concentrating on the matter of dying, but showing no anguish. He even retained his cheerfulness when von Westermann, the Berlin Philharmonic *Intendant*, came to see him. Furtwängler said goodbye to him and told him to give his greetings and best wishes to his orchestra. Westermann burst into tears, but Furtwängler changed the subject quickly and started to discuss changes he wished to make in the programmes of the forthcoming tour of America in January 1955. After Westermann had gone he said to his wife with a smile: 'Did you notice how I stopped him from crying?'

On 30 November 1954, after the blood transfusion, Frau Elisabeth sat on the edge of her Wilhelm's bed, holding his hand. Suddenly he pulled her arm across his chest, raised himself slightly, took a deep breath, fell back into his pillows and died.

He found his last resting place, as he had wished, on the *Bergfriedhof* in Heidelberg.

Soon after her return to Clarens, Ansermet visited Frau Elisabeth and asked about his end. Elisabeth told him that in dying Furtwängler had taught her that the acceptance of death was an aim to strive for. After a pause Ansermet replied: 'Yes – but one must know how to do it. *He knew!*'

8

Conclusion

Furtwängler was dead. Outside Germany the event was hardly noticed, and some newspapers saw fit to rake up the old dirt about his 'Nazi associations' and offer criticism of his 'subjectivity'. The musical press was more generous and paid tribute to the loss of a genius. Letters of condolence from great musicians and others poured in from all over the world. There were a number of memorial concerts. His colleague and friend Sir Thomas Beecham took over the two concerts he was to have conducted in London on 18 and 20 January 1955 in the Royal Festival Hall with the Royal Philharmonic. Beecham retained the programmes Furtwängler had laid down without change, though they can hardly have been to his taste. Before the first concert on 18 January 1955 he addressed the audience briefly as follows:

> I shall not speak to you tonight about Wilhelm Furtwängler's musicianship. You know enough about that. He was a fine musician and a man of the highest integrity. In the difficult times in Germany he protected the weak and assisted the helpless. My tribute is to a man of remarkable and sterling character, and we see very few of them anywhere in these days.

The greatest memorial concert came in 1956 when Keilberth conducted Furtwängler's Symphony No.3 for the first time in Berlin. As we noted, Furtwängler had jotted down titles for the four movements. When she returned to Clarens Frau Elisabeth found the score open on the piano. In pencil he had written these headings over the first *three* movements – but the title of the fourth was omitted, for Furtwängler was not satisfied with it.

8. Conclusion

After long discussions Frau Elisabeth and Keilberth decided to omit the Finale and let the symphony stand, like Bruckner's Ninth, as a three-movement torso. It was probably the best solution, as Brian Wright's performance of all four movements in the BBC studios on 10 July 1983 has proved: it was interesting to hear the sketch of the Finale, but it was unworthy of Furtwängler, and the experiment ought not to be repeated.

During the last years of his life the great Austrian painter Oskar Kokoschka, who had lived in exile in London until 1952, settled on Lake Geneva close to the Furtwänglers. The two men became friends, united by a common artistic outlook. As late as the summer and autumn of 1954 they discussed Kokoschka's designs of costumes and scenery for the *Magic Flute* which Furtwängler was to conduct in Salzburg in 1955. The authorities there agreed. Kokoschka was enthusiastic and made the designs, but in 1955 and 1956 it was up to Solti to conduct the performances. I have been told too that it was Kokoschka's intention to paint a portrait of Furtwängler. He had studied his walk, his hands, his legs, his posture in detail and had prepared a canvas. The canvas remained blank, leaning against the wall of his studio for years.

As often happens with *performing* musicians, Furtwängler's renown waned. He had never been a man keen to work in the studio, and in the English catalogue his studio recordings were deleted one after the other, until only *Tristan* remained. This was the period when stereo became popular. All record collectors went stereo-mad, and of course Furtwängler's commercial recordings were all in mono. This may have been a subsidiary reason for the neglect and consequent deletion of his recorded repertoire. But in the late 1950s Electrola began to issue records of his live concerts. The tenth anniversary of his death in 1964 marked a turning point. The event was commemorated in many places, including London. On 30 November 1964 the Royal Philharmonic gave a memorial concert for Furtwängler in the Royal Albert Hall, which I was privileged to conduct.

In 1967 a Wilhelm Furtwängler Society was formed in Great Britain, and others followed in America, France, Germany and Switzerland. Their main purpose was to stimulate interest in Furtwängler's achievements by persuading companies to reissue recordings which had been deleted and make available recordings of live concerts which were stored in private archives. Since the 1960s we have had a spate of issues – some official, some pirated – and there is now a mass of Furtwängler recordings and a huge congregation of Furtwängler admirers all over the world. It is gratifying that Furtwängler's influence, through the medium of the gramophone record, is reaching so many young musicians. This is paradoxical, for Furtwängler himself was fundamentally opposed to all forms of mechanical reproduction. Yet who does not wish that there were recordings of Wagner, Richter, Levi conducting? Many even listen to recordings of Muck or Nikisch, bad though the reproduction may be. The age of satisfactory mechanical reproduction only began in the time of Furtwängler and Toscanini, to mention but two of the great conductors, and we must consider ourselves lucky that we can still listen to their music in this way.

We possess the heritage, but it is sad nevertheless that the number of those who knew Furtwängler personally and were privileged to hear him on the podium, experiencing the extraordinary musical personality that emanated from him, is gradually dwindling as time passes. Yet it is gratifying to see how his reputation keeps rising *posthumously* more than any conductor's before.

In 1945, aged 81, Richard Strauss wrote to Joseph Gregor voicing the hope that 'if there [was] any new territory at all to be explored in that field, [his] operas might prove to be good building material on the "Avenue of Sphinxes" '. Let us hope that the recorded legacy of Furtwängler may prove in the same way to be a row of sphinxes sign-posting the path for a younger generation.

9

The Personality of Furtwängler

Furtwängler is acknowledged to have been a musical genius. But people often take genius as an isolated facet of a person and expect him to be a perfectly ordinary man in other respects. This obviously cannot be, and Furtwängler's personality in day-to-day matters was as complex as his musical self.

It is often said that Furtwängler was sentimental and arrogant. That he had sentiment there can be no doubt – we have only to listen to his performances and compositions – but there was no sentimentality whatever in his make-up. The best proof is that in his letters and writings there is hardly any mention of his innermost feelings, and he steadfastly refused to write an autobiography. As for arrogance, where is the borderline between arrogance and self-assurance? Is it arrogant that he delighted in the applause that greeted him at the end of a concert? Does not every performing artist relish his reception by the public? There is another side to this 'arrogance': many great artists give the outward impression of arrogance because they are basically shy and protect themselves with a sort of defensive armour. Furtwängler knew this. When, after 1952, he became increasingly worried about his hearing, he consulted a psychiatrist who gave him a questionnaire containing the question 'Are you shy?' Furtwängler answered: 'Very shy, except in front of the orchestra.' In private he was modest, as is shown by the following story. In the early 1930s – when he and the great actor Gustav Gründgens were the virtual artistic kings of Berlin, known to everyone by sight – there was a reception. A friend of mine was there who did not know anyone – like another guest whom, of course, he immediately recognised as Furtwängler. The two got into a casual conversation, as outsiders on such occasions often do. After they had exchanged a few words the other man said: 'Forgive me, I haven't introduced myself. My name is Furtwängler.' I remember reading that, in such a situation, it is the prerogative of the very great to take it for granted that everybody knows who they are, but it is only the half-great who make use of the privilege. Furtwängler could be infuriated by bad press reviews. It is a matter of individuality. Some artists, with a greater sense of the ridiculous, can shrug off a bad press notice with a grin, because they can judge their own performance themselves. Furtwängler could not, and such reviews irked him. But he was honest with himself, as I can attest. Once when I went to see him in the artists' room after a Beethoven concert and presented myself to him, the last in the queue, he looked at me sadly and said: 'Please don't say how wonderful it was – I know it was bad.' I remember saying to him: 'I know you weren't at your best – but even so it was ten times better than what we are accustomed to hear from others.' All this is well summed up by Piatigorsky in his autobiography (*Gregor Piatigorsky, Cellist*, New York, 1965):

> Furtwängler had a contradictory nature. He was ambitious and jealous, noble and vain, coward and hero, strong and weak, a child and a man of wisdom, both very German and yet a man of the world. He was one only in music, undivided and unique.

We have already seen that in his youth Furtwängler was self-opinionated and domineering, and could not bear losing. Karla Höcker (p.31) adds another dimension:

> One day when Willi was about eight or ten he sat in a room in Munich, reading. He was rapt. The maid came in to set the table and told him that he would have to stop, but he was so engrossed in his book that he did not budge. Finally she took it away from him and went through a glass door into the next room to put it down, closing the door behind her. Willi rushed out in a fury, head first through that glass door, thereby cutting his cheek severely. In many a photo this scar is still clearly visible.

Naturally in the course of time he learnt to curb his temper, but occasionally his innate hot-headedness would break through, as in his telephone conversation with Himmler mentioned earlier.

After slamming down the receiver his temper got the better of him, and he furiously pounded the window. His fist proved stronger than the pane and he was rewarded by a nasty gash. In rehearsal he was most amenable, kind and understanding with his orchestra, for he felt himself to be one of them. He only rarely lost his patience, but when he *did* ... ! I was present at one of these outbursts. He had gone over a certain passage several times when he suddenly threw down his baton and slunk off the podium muttering: 'Well, if you can't play it the way I want it I might as well go home.' In our democratic days few orchestras would tolerate such behaviour in a conductor, but from Furtwängler they took it. They sat there like a bunch of schoolboys who had been scolded by the headmaster, till the leader went to the artists' room and smoothed his ruffled feathers. Furtwängler returned and continued the rehearsal, and all was well again. There was a similar outburst in 1952 during the recording sessions of *Tristan und Isolde* which led to the final break with Walter Legge, but of this we shall hear later. Furtwängler must have been aware of this shortcoming in his character, however, as is shown by a trivial story told by Frau Elisabeth. They had been somewhere – it is immaterial where – and had returned to their car in the car park. Frau Elisabeth was upset about something and when they got to the car battered the bonnet with her fists, hurting her hands. Furtwängler just smiled at her and said gently: 'Yes, I understand – and afterwards one feels so ashamed, doesn't one?'

We have noted that Furtwängler was no socialite. He detested receptions and cocktail parties, much preferring to be in a convivial circle of musicians and others discussing philosophical and artistic problems. In the great world of high society he was a stranger and rather gauche. Again I must quote Frau Elisabeth. They had been invited to some big affair – an ambassadorial dinner or the like – and one of the guests remarked: 'Isn't it lovely! It's all Meissen china.' Furtwängler replied: 'Yes, we have Meissen at home too, but ours is all chipped!' – a remark which must have been embarrassing for his wife at the time. Yet I have my suspicions. Furtwängler was such an intelligent and cultured man: did he really make such remarks inadvertently, or with his tongue in his cheek? Was he committing a *faux-pas*,

at his wedding to Elisabeth in 1943) and John Knittel, though with him one has the impression that it was a little forced.

He was most at his ease with children, particularly his own. He had the gift of retaining a child-like freshness in himself and therefore of being able to understand the souls of persons much younger than himself. He liked the relaxation of playing with them in the garden, and their noise never worried him. Frau Elisabeth tells of a day when the children were roller-skating on the terrace just outside the room he was working in, making such a racket that she herself was incapable of writing a simple letter. Furtwängler was quite unaware of it all and even told her off when she tried to restrain them, saying: 'Children never disturb me – it is only adults that bother me!' On another occasion, Frau Elisabeth remarked that her children always were the loudest, to which he replied with a smile: 'Not surprising – after all, they are *yours*.' This innate love of the young is best expressed in his letters. For instance, he wrote to his daughter Friederike from London when she was about seventeen:

> Some day we must have a good talk about your worries as to what you are going to do in the future. For the moment I will just say that one shouldn't worry about such things before one has to. When the time is ripe one thinks further ahead, and in most cases the right direction finds itself quite naturally. Only very few people know at your age what they really want to become, and it is very good that way.

Then, about a year later, he wrote to her from Copenhagen:

> Do write to me again, e.g. what you have done during the Easter holidays. And when the day comes that you fall in love with someone you must tell me that too – don't you think so?
> I am counting the days till all this conducting is finished and I can get down to my own work. Love to your Mummy. To you, my darling, a big kiss.

His relationship with his youngest daughter Almut was no less charming and understanding, but it would go too far to quote all his letters to her.

Furtwängler had a deep feeling for family life. He always tried to help his mother, his brother and his sisters, both humanly and materially. It is touching to read what Frau Elisabeth has to say on the subject in her book (p.145). At the time they were already in Switzerland, and she only had her youngest child from her first marriage there, the other three being still with relatives in Germany. Naturally, in those days of poor communications, this was a constant worry to her. Then, one night, knowing that she was lying awake, he said to her: 'I must tell you that I know very well what oppresses you, even if you never speak of it. You must not lose faith: we shall all be reunited – I shall do everything humanly possible to make it come about.' It is touching that he considered himself and *his* children, Frau Elisabeth and *her* children, and their own son Andreas, as one big family.

I once asked Frau Elisabeth what Furtwängler did when he had one or more days free from conducting. Her reply was that he composed and went for long walks. But of course no person can live like that all the time. His delight in playing with children has been mentioned. He also liked to go to the cinema sometimes, or read a thriller, but that was about all. While he loved sport in all its forms, it was walking that was essential to him. His slouch has often been remarked upon. A friend of mine, John Hillaby, who spent most of his life walking and mountaineering, has the same sort of gait as Furtwängler.

Apart from all this Furtwängler was an avid reader and devoured books on his travels, whether in trains or on planes. His heroes were Homer, Shakespeare and Goethe. Strangely he had no great feeling for Schiller; his favourite German dramatists were Kleist and Grillparzer. He was also susceptible to modern literature, not only to German authors, but also to English, Irish and American. He read Joyce's *Ulysses* and was moved by Hemingway's *The Old Man and the Sea*. But he had little rapport with Proust and Rilke. Though Mann was so hostile to him after his emigration, he admired Mann greatly. The last work of Mann's he read was probably *Doktor Faustus*, which he appreciated, but he remarked: 'Thomas Mann is a Wagnerian, and there he is at home musically. About Beethoven's Op.111 he really shouldn't talk so much – but then, one doesn't have to know everything.' Kant, Schopenhauer, Nietzsche were his constant companions. When in 1947 the composer and conductor Eugène Goossens became the Director of the NSW State Conservatorium of Music in Sydney he summoned a colloquium of all the students, of which I was one. In his address Goossens made two points, which I shall never forget. One was that, as musicians, we had not a forty-hour week, but a fourteen-hour day, a seven-day week and a 52-week year. The other was that we not only had to know our music but were also artists in general. As such it was our duty to be conversant with all the arts: literature, architecture, painting and so on. Furtwängler fulfilled both these tenets.

In his diet he was selective but basically undemanding. He did not touch alcohol – except at official receptions where courtesy demanded that he at least take a sip of champagne – nor did he drink coffee. Yet he needed a large amount of liquid – milk, mineral water, fruit juice, herb tea – and he loved yoghurt. He ate sparingly, and very little meat. At times he was a complete vegetarian, insisting on biodynamically grown fruit and vegetables, just as he was inclined to homoeopathic medicines. When at home he ate whatever Lenchen, or later Frau Elisabeth, prepared for him, but in restaurants he could be difficult and spend hours studying the menu. Frau Elisabeth has much to tell about this. Sometimes he would order something unfamiliar, just because the name appealed to him. Invariably, when the food was served, he decided that what Elisabeth had ordered was better, and so plates had to be exchanged. On one occasion she saw grilled liver on the menu, a dish she had not had for a long time, and when she ordered it she told him that, no matter what, this time she would eat what she had chosen. Furtwängler was positively affronted. Once, when lunching at a high-class restaurant, he threw the staff into confusion by calmly ordering a bowl of porridge. On another occasion, when he was having breakfast with a journalist at an airport before departure, he ordered a glass of milk and a plate. He emptied half a jar of jam onto the plate, poured the milk over it, stirred it all up – and that was his breakfast. When I told Frau Elisabeth these stories she said: 'Well, I wasn't present, but it sounds typical.' What a far cry from the young man of the Lübeck days who spent free afternoons wallowing in cakes and whipped cream in the cafés! He had one particular habit: just before leaving for a concert he would eat a raw egg. By then he was in full evening dress, and he would pierce a hole at each end of the egg and drink it out of the shell. It terrified Frau Elisabeth, but he had the knack of it, and the dreaded sight of yolk down his shirt front was always averted.

In his dress he was unconventional – except, of course, for his evening dress, about which he was always most meticulous. Otherwise, for many years, he left it all to the faithful Lenchen. She probably knew him better than any other person between the time he left his mother and the advent of Frau Elisabeth. She looked after everything, including his clothes, and she always knew what was in his mind. Like most men, Furtwängler was addicted to certain clothes and would continue wearing them even when they were ripe for the dustbin. At one time he was attached to a little Tyrolean hat which had seen better days. Coming back from a walk one day he said to Lenchen: 'I suppose this hat is rather shabby? People have looked at me so strangely – should I throw it away?' Lenchen said no, for she knew it would have broken his heart if she had said yes. Generally he wore hats which looked as though somebody had accidentally sat on them. Then there was his raincoat ... ! Anyone who saw him after a concert in the artists' room putting on his raincoat over his tails will know what I mean. I would claim that his was the most disreputable raincoat ever – if I had not seen Klemperer's.

We have already noted in the Lübeck period Furtwängler's prowess as a dancer: on the floor he seemed to gyrate in a slightly lunatic fashion, and his concept of dancing seems to have been along the lines of the French dictum – *Ce n'est pas pour le rythme, c'est pour le frôlement*. In all their years together Frau Elisabeth only once ventured onto the dance floor with him – that was enough. It is a fact that most musicians are bad dancers: somehow they seem to have rhythm in their arms, their hands, but not in their feet. Piatigorsky tells an amusing story of the days when they were both in Berlin:

Neither of us knew how to dance, so Furtwängler and I had decided to take lessons. With assumed names, we entered the class. After the third lesson the teacher said that we were exceptional cases and, being unmusical, had better have the special course. We gave it up altogether.

In the late 1920s or so Furtwängler acquired a car and also managed to acquire a driving licence. His Berlin friends – such as are still alive – wonder to this day how he succeeded in passing his test, for he always confused the brake and the accelerator. A few days later, after conducting at the Berlin State Opera, Richard Strauss came up to him in the artists' room and they decided to have dinner together at the Hotel Adlon, not far from the Opera. I cannot do better than quote Curt Riess (p.90):

> Furtwängler said in an off-hand manner: 'My car is just outside. We can go.' Strauss, ever suspicious, asked: 'You drive yourself?' Furtwängler replied with the mien of a man who had been driving for years: 'But of course.' A few minutes later the car was speeding in the direction of Hotel Adlon, was still speeding a few yards before reaching the hotel and, far worse, as it was approaching the white Mercedes of Prince Reuss. 'Why don't you brake?' shouted Strauss. But then Furtwängler probably didn't know exactly which was the brake. Possibly he accelerated. In any case he hit the white car of Prince Reuss with a resounding bang. Strauss said: 'What a nincompoop!' The remarks of Prince Reuss have not been recorded, but the fact remains that, for the rest of his life, Strauss refused to get into any car if Furtwängler was behind the wheel.

There were other occasions fraught with peril, such as when he was in a car with Karla Höcker. While expounding Goethe's philosophy he completely overlooked a red light. Brakes squealed, a policeman lumbered across, saw who was driving, grinned, and waved him on. Furtwängler's only comment was: 'Dash it – it's all Goethe's fault.'

To do him justice, he later became an excellent driver, though always on the fast side. When I discussed the subject with Frau Elisabeth she agreed: 'Yes, he was an excellent driver, except when he began talking about music. Then he took his hands off the wheel and began conducting. Also, he was impossible when *I* was driving and *he* was the passenger, always telling me when I could overtake and when not. On the other hand, when *he* was at the wheel he took no notice of anything, overtook whenever he felt like it and simply said: "When I overtake, nobody comes the other way." '

Hans Geiger, a violinist in the Philharmonia Orchestra during Furtwängler's tour to the Lucerne Festival in 1954, told me a good story: Furtwängler's hotel lay in the same direction, and after the morning rehearsal Geiger (himself no slow driver) drove back to where he was staying on the north side of Lake Lucerne, a road notorious for its curves. Suddenly he was overtaken by Furtwängler, driving even faster. In the evening, before the concert, he asked Furtwängler's secretary: 'Does he always drive that fast?' She replied: 'No, not normally, but he said to me: "That's one of the members of the orchestra in front of me, and they always say I do everything so slowly!".'

Money was an alien world to Furtwängler. This was not only because his mind was on higher things. Until his father's death in 1907 he lived mostly with his family. They were not particularly rich, but they were comfortably off. Then came the early years to 1911, when he was an apprentice conductor in Zürich, Munich and Strasbourg and his salary was not very high. These were the only years – apart from 1945-47 which we have already discussed – when he may have felt short of money. But in 1911, at the age of 25, he became the chief conductor of the Lübeck orchestra, and in 1915 he was appointed *Hofkapellmeister* at the Opera in Mannheim. I have not been able to discover what his income was in either of these positions, but it can't have been negligible. The patrician town of Lübeck and the old musical centre of Mannheim would have paid their leading conductor a salary commensurate with his position and responsibility. In 1922 he became the chief conductor of the two most prominent orchestras in Germany – in Leipzig and Berlin – and his combined income from these sources must have been substantial. We may conclude therefore that he must have been fairly well off financially up to 1945 and from 1947 onwards for, in addition to his salaries, he must have had a fairly large income from his guest engagements. It is silly to say therefore, as some do, that Furtwängler was not interested in money; that, when offered an engagement, he was interested only in the programme, the quality of the orchestra, the accoustics of the hall and the like. Obviously nobody would offer him trifling fees, and it is relatively easy to ignore financial considerations when one has enough to fall back on.

Furtwängler was extraordinarily generous to his mother, his brother and sisters and his friends, especially his refugee friends during the Nazi era. In an interview on Radio Hilversum in 1986 (the 100th anniversary of Furtwängler's birth) the noted Berlin musicologist and critic Hans Heinz Stuckenschmidt (of whom we shall say more later) made *inter alia* the following remarks regarding Furtwängler and money:

> Furtwängler could always dispose of considerable means. ... One of his most important characteristics was his *noblesse*. He was a noble person, noble in his mind, noble in financial matters ... The only person who surpassed him in material generosity was Yehudi Menuhin.

Furtwängler's complete ignorance and nonchalance in money matters led to some amusing incidents. Often he boarded a tram and found he had no money. Usually some kind conductor paid the fare for him, but Furtwängler always took the man's name and address and never forgot to repay him. Similarly, at the taxi rank near the *Fasanerie* he was known as 'that tall chap who never has any money on him'. But this attitude to material values could have more serious consequences. As we have noted, Furtwängler resigned from the Berlin Philharmonicin 1934 for political reasons and after the war, although pressed, refused to sign another contract until December 1951. This meant that he was only a salaried member of staff for the years 1922-34 and for the last three years of his life. This inevitably had a disastrous effect on his pension rights. He just did not have the type of mind to grasp the importance of such things, and his wife had to bear the brunt of it after his death. Granted, the Berlin Philharmonic gave her an 'honorary stipend', but that hardly amounted to much. By contrast, Herbert von Karajan had much better business acumen. When he was appointed Furtwängler's successor he made sure that it was a contract for life.

Furtwängler's basic German mentality has been referred to often enough, as well as the conflict it caused him during the years of Nazism, confronting him again and again with the decision whether to emigrate or stand by his country in its hour of direst need. Yes, he *was* a German. He had his roots in German soil and gathered all his strength from German nature, German philosophy, German art. But two things must be considered. One is that these roots were in the Germany of the nineteenth century when slogans such as 'German faith' and 'Germany, the land of poets and thinkers' were no more arrogant than the English 'My country right or wrong'. Furtwängler was no more jingoistically a German than Chopin was a Pole, Dvořák a Czech, Debussy a Frenchman, or Vaughan Williams an Englishman. Several diary entries have already been quoted, but it is perhaps worth citing two letters from long before the days of Hitler: to Curtius from Stockholm in 1920 and to Curtius's wife Edith from St Moritz in 1923:

> People here are very strange, not in their relation to music and the so-called 'intellectual' interests which only appear to be superficial, but in their relation to nature, to love. I can only say one thing: I am always proud and happy to be a German. What that means one only comes to realise when one is abroad.

> But to a certain extent I believe in something like providence, destiny. Only one should recognise that acting or, more precisely, being forced to act, can also be providence. In this sense I must always think of Germany and its present terrible political situation.

It is always difficult when discussing a great personality to talk about religion, for this is to enter the realms of the innermost self. Let us first state the facts. Both Furtwängler's parents were of Protestant stock, and he was baptised in the Lutheran faith. We know little about his mother's religion, but his father's was undoubtedly a mixture of staunch Lutheranism and Classical ideals. It was he who insisted that the boy went to Sunday School, though when Willi returned he was apt to ask with a sardonic smile: 'Well, what lies did those parsons tell you today?'

Furtwängler was a deeply religious person. We only have to listen to his recordings of the St Matthew Passion or Bruckner's Ninth to realise it. But he was no church-goer, no conformist – spiritually he stood far above any form of organised religion. As with everything in life, he saw things from a philosophical angle. Gradually, apart from the background he had inherited from his father, he studied the philosophical aspects of religion and became interested in Theosophy and Anthroposophy. In fact he read a great deal of Rudolf Steiner. He never put his thoughts on paper, and we can only gather his ideas in a fragmentary way. For instance, when Weingartner died in 1942 he was aghast that he had stipulated in his will that the final duet from Verdi's *Aida* should be sung at his funeral. When he told this to his future wife she asked him spontaneously: 'What would you like to be played at your funeral?' He answered equally spontaneously: 'The Chorale *Wenn ich einmal soll scheiden* from Bach's St Matthew Passion' – sure proof that he had already given the matter some thought.

Wilhelm and Elisabeth were married in 1943 in a register office. In November 1945, when their son Andreas was almost a year old, Frau Elisabeth suggested that it was high time for him to be baptised. Furtwängler objected: 'But dearest, we haven't even been married in church.' Actually this would have been no objection, but Furtwängler insisted. So they were duly married in a little church in Montreux, and the baby was christened. For Furtwängler marriage was a sacrament.

Once, in 1948, when Furtwängler and his wife were flying from Rio to Buenos Aires there was a shaky take-off and people screamed. Frau Elisabeth was very perturbed. He looked at her and said: 'Dearest, are you afraid?' She could not deny it. He said calmly, confidently: 'We are all in God's hands.'

Finally, we may quote from a letter to Max Auer, President of the International Bruckner Society, from Clarens on 12 November 1952. Bruckner IX had always had a supreme place in Furtwängler's estimation:

Which work in symphonic literature deserves more than Bruckner's Ninth Symphony to be heard in church? The performance of this incomparable work which I conducted during the last and worst phase of the war in the church of St Florian will remain indelible in my memory. [This performance on 11 October 1944 was, I believe, the last time that Furtwängler ever conducted Bruckner's Ninth.] I think in all sincerity I could suggest to the Holy Father that this grandiose work should be officially acknowledged as a sacred work.

Lastly, we must consider Furtwängler's attitude to his colleagues. When asked for an opinion he could be very critical and outspoken. This was often not appreciated, and he once declared, furious with himself at his own honesty: 'In future I shall do it like many of my colleagues. After every performance they have heard they say it was "ravishing".' Unfortunately Furtwängler could not stick to this resolution. But he was exceedingly fair. He knew no malice, and never bore a grudge. To give a few examples: he was on good terms with Klemperer from his Strasbourg days and often went on mountain walks with him, discussing musical problems. He respected Klemperer, even though the two men never met again after they were separated by the political events that followed 1933. Then there was Bruno Walter, whom Furtwängler met as a young man and who was instrumental in his obtaining the post in Mannheim in 1915. Though they disagreed at times on musical and political questions, there was always a personal friendship, a human relationship between the two men. Walter sided with Furtwängler in the Chicago affair, and when they met again after the war they settled their differences.

About Toscanini and Menuhin enough has been said. Knappertsbusch and Kleiber were both good friends of Furtwängler's. There was the incident when Knappertsbusch in 1943 conducted *Siegfried* at the Vienna State Opera. At the beginning of the second act Knappertsbusch rushed onto the rostrum and began without looking at the orchestra properly. In the sixth bar there was no tuba, and subsequently it became obvious that the First Trumpet was also missing. In Frau Elisabeth's words:

> He had to stop and wait for the brass players who, apparently, had not heard the bell for the end of the intermission. He was furious and swore that he would never conduct the Vienna Philharmonic again. The management of the orchestra could not calm him down – in fact, he would not even talk to them. Furtwängler was conducting concerts in Vienna at that time, and so the management came to him and begged him insistently to intervene with Knappertsbusch, asking for forgiveness on behalf of the sinners. Furtwängler did so and managed to placate him. However, at his next rehearsal he could not forbear to say to the orchestra with a broad grin: 'Well, one always has to have a good look to make sure all the Professors are sitting at their desks!'

In the case of Kleiber the matter was not so funny. As may be remembered, soon after Furtwängler laid down his musical offices in Berlin in December 1934 on political grounds, Kleiber resigned out of solidarity and emigrated to South America, though he was neither Jewish nor otherwise 'undesirable'. In 1951 he came back to Berlin and became musical director of the East Berlin State Opera, a fact which caused much adverse comment in the West German press. Furtwängler went to hear his first performance. When the applause had died down, he rose from his seat in the stalls and made a deep bow to Kleiber to acknowledge that he also had performed a courageous deed despite the unpopularity it entailed.

There remains, however, one very contentious issue: the relationship between Furtwängler and Karajan. This has been greatly overstressed by Walter Legge. In the course of a symposium on Furtwängler on 30 November 1964 (the tenth anniversary of his death) on the BBC Third Programme, Walter Legge described Furtwängler as 'desperately jealous'. Jealous, yes – desperately, no. Furtwängler was no more jealous of Karajan than any conductor, pianist, violinist or singer is jealous of an up-and-coming rival. Furtwängler was perfectly fair, even though he and Karajan had nothing whatever in common in humanity, philosophy, attitude to money, and even music. He recognised Karajan's undoubted abilities, however, and on 31 January 1950 he wrote to Ernst Fischer, the chairman of the committee of the Berlin Philharmonic Orchestra:

> I can only applaud the intentions about which you wrote to me. I find it absolutely necessary that Karajan, when he comes to Berlin, should be a guest with your orchestra and not at the State Opera.

Two years later, on 2 April 1952, he wrote to Fischer again:

> I would suggest that Celibidache and Karajan should be offered as many concerts as they wish, time permitting.

and shortly afterwards:

> Especially I feel that the relation of the conductors is not right, i.e. not according to their importance. If a man like Celibidache gets six concerts, it is hard to understand that Schuricht, Jochum, etc. get only one or two. Especially Karajan, whose name is greater than that of C., must also be offered six. And from *our* side: I attach great importance to that.

The arch-demon was Walter Legge. He was the absolute boss of what was then HMV and Columbia in the UK. He was an autocrat, perhaps one of the ablest men the recording industry has ever seen, and a great producer; but his human qualities are open to question. Go-getter that he was, he latched on to Furtwängler at first but later decided to put his money on Karajan. In the summer of 1947 he tried to pour oil on troubled

137

waters by arranging a dinner at which Furtwängler and Karajan with their wives and the general secretary of the *Gesellschaft der Musikfreunde* of Vienna, Rudolf Gamsjäger, were present. According to the memoirs[1] collated by his wife Elisabeth Schwarzkopf the dinner was a fiasco and resulted in permanent enmity between Furtwängler and Karajan. How is it then that, as Frau Elisabeth relates, Karajan and his wife had dinner at the Furtwänglers', just the four of them, in Salzburg in 1948? How is it that, when there was trouble about transport the next day, Karajan volunteered to drive the Furtwänglers to the railway station? One should never exaggerate. Elisabeth Schwarzkopf says that, according to Walter Legge, 'Furtwängler's resentment toward Herbert von Karajan was quite irrational, to the degree that he was unable to pronounce his name! ("This man K!").' Legge, being an Englishman, may well not have seen this in the right light, but Madame Schwarzkopf as a German, knowing the habits of Berliners and their love of abbreviating things, should have realised that referring to Karajan as 'K' or 'von K' was no more derogatory than referring, as they did, to Knappertsbusch as 'Kna' and Furtwängler as 'Fu'.

The relationship between Furtwängler and Walter Legge is a different matter. Legge had suggested to Furtwängler after his performance of *Zauberflöte* in Salzburg in 1949 that they should record it. Furtwängler conducted *Die Zauberflöte* again in Salzburg in 1950 and 1951. In November 1950, Legge recorded it with Karajan with the same orchestra, the same chorus, virtually the same soloists. It is not surprising that Furtwängler had every reason to hate Walter Legge. The crunch came in 1952 when Furtwängler recorded the complete *Tristan* in Kingsway Hall, London. Legge was the producer. Now Furtwängler was a conductor who did not want to be interfered with, even in recordings, and Legge was a person who insisted on interfering with artists. In one of the sessions Furtwängler went off to hear a playback. What exactly transpired is not known, but we *do* know that Furtwängler stormed out of the recording room in a fury, donning the aforementioned disreputable raincoat, and vanished into the street, though there was still half an hour of

[1] Elisabeth Schwarzkopf, *On and Off the Record: A Memoir of Walter Legge* (London 1982).

the session to go. This on the verbal authority of Hans Geiger and the written testimony of Manoug Parikian, the leader of the Philharmonia Orchestra. When the *Tristan* recording was completed they had two sessions in hand. As Fischer-Dieskau, the *Kurwenal* in the recording, was still available Legge suggested that they should use these to record Mahler's *Lieder eines fahrenden Gesellen*. Furtwängler agreed, but insisted on another producer. Lawrance Collingwood produced. He remained Furtwängler's producer for all HMV records he made to the end of his life including the very last, the studio recording of *Walküre*.

There is one other colleague to be discussed, though he is not a conductor: Hans Heinz Stuckenschmidt (1901-1988), probably the greatest critic and writer on music in the German-speaking countries since Hanslick, odious though he might have found this comparison. He was 31 when the Nazis came to power. By Nazi standards he was 'Aryan', but he was distinctly leftist, defending the *avant-garde* such as Schoenberg, Berg, and Webern, and his wife was Jewish. Early in 1932 Furtwängler published an article in which he attacked certain aspects of contemporary music and musical life. Stuckenschmidt replied sharply, and a journalistic duel resulted between the two men though they had never met face to face. Their first meeting came about in Bayreuth in the summer. Furtwängler, when introduced to Stuckenschmidt, said in his pointedly brusque manner: 'So that's what you look like.' They then talked for fifteen or twenty minutes. They disagreed on many essential things, but they came to respect each other's integrity – for Stuckenschmidt admired Furtwängler as a conductor, even when he objected to his romanticising aesthetics – and they found a basis in what might be called a loose acquaintanceship. Things changed with Hitler. Stuckenschmidt refused to adapt himself to the new regime and continued to say openly what he thought right. Consequently he lost his position as the chief critic of the Berlin daily *BZ am Mittag*, for he was debarred from joining the *Reichskulturkammer* ('State Board of Culture') and expelled from the *Reichsschrifttumskammer* ('State Board of Writers'). His circumstances became precarious, and in 1935 he applied for readmission to the Board of Writers. I said earlier

10

Furtwängler the Musician

It must not be forgotten that Furtwängler was essentially a man of the nineteenth century. Born in 1886, he was already 14 when the twentieth century officially began; but in reality it did not begin until the outbreak of the First World War in 1914, by which time he was 28. Then there was the strong influence of his father, who was born in 1853, clearly a nineteenth-century man, as were the most influential personalities in his upbringing: Curtius (born 1874), Riezler (born 1878), Rheinberger (born 1839), von Schillings (born 1868) and others. With this background why accuse Furtwängler of looking back to the nineteenth century, the era of romanticism? There is also a conundrum: was he a composer/conductor or a conductor/composer? Many composers fall into one or other of these categories. Weingartner, Klemperer, Rafael Kubelik, to name but three, were, or are, highly proficient composers, but in the main we revere them as conductors. Richard Strauss, Hindemith and Benjamin Britten were great conductors, but posterity will ever remember them as the fine composers they were. With Mahler (1860-1911) the case is somewhat different. There are no extant recordings of Mahler as a conductor, but from what I am told by the few friends of mine who were still alive and old enough to have heard him, such as Hans Gál (1890-1987), his abilities as a conductor must have been outstanding. Mahler's case is often quoted by those who contend that Furtwängler was a conductor first and only secondarily a composer. True, Mahler's output of compositions far exceeds that of Furtwängler, and when he died he was only 51, whereas

Furtwängler lived to 68. But Mahler lived and worked in different times. In his day there was the concert and opera season from autumn to late spring or early summer, but there were no festivals, so that performing musicians had a long holiday in the summer during which they could devote themselves to their other interests. How different when we look at Furtwängler's time-table, spending the summer months rushing from Edinburgh to Lucerne, to Bayreuth, to Salzburg.

From the age of seven or eight Furtwängler declared himself to be a composer, and he said so repeatedly in his letters. Granted, he composed many pieces, but later he rejected most of them. Probably the first work to which he accorded any validity is the *Te Deum* of 1909. He disavowed more of his compositions than he sanctioned. The list of his works (below, pp. 170-3) gives some indication. Is it not fair, then, to assume that a man so dedicated to composing, so sure that he was destined to be a composer, would not have found the way, the means, to liberate himself from his conducting obligations in order to compose? There were others who were not affluent, who gave up their salaried positions, because they needed the time to compose. Furtwängler did not. It is all very well to say that he was a person who could not say 'no', but if he had been so deeply devoted to his vocation he could have said 'no' at times. Then there is the time-scale of his works: there is hardly one which is less than an hour long. To contrive works of that length requires the genius of a Bruckner, and Furtwängler did not have that ultimate genius as a composer. His music is perfectly constructed, perfectly knowledgeable and craftsman-like in every respect; but to me, and I am being honest, he is unable to sustain the tension of the enormous spans he is trying to encompass – with the possible exception of his Symphonic Piano Concerto, and the unfinished Third Symphony where he indeed touches spiritual heights. He was in a continual dilemma, as his letters show. From Bayreuth he wrote to Curtius (undated, August 1931?):

> That probably was the greatest mistake of my life – that my destiny and my profession shackled me to Berlin, whereas in solitude I could have become that which I believed I *had* to become. Only – do I still believe it now?

Yet two years or so before his death (in 1952, according to Riess, p.315) he wrote in a letter:

> At ten o'clock in the evening, after the concert, the activity of the conductor is over. Later they can tell all sorts of lies about the concert. For that reason it is an activity which is built on sand ... In order to survive, one single creative work of art is more important than all the activity of a conductor. That is why composing appears so much more essential to me – for after all, composing and conducting flow from the same source. Unfortunately worldly circumstances seduced me to give too little time to this task and now, because of the serious illness which my body had to conquer, I am being reminded of this omission.

Furtwängler was a composer of the utmost sincerity and integrity. Indeed Arthur Honegger wrote after his death:

> The man who wrote a score as rich as his Second Symphony cannot be discussed. He is of the race of great musicians.

Furtwängler continually revised, emended, improved. He was a perfectionist. In that sense he was like Bruckner. He was also somewhat similar to Ravel, who once said in a lecture in Houston in 1928:

> In my own compositions I judge a long period of conscious gestation necessary. During this interval I come progressively, and with growing precision, to see the form and the evolution that the final work will take in its totality. Thus I can be occupied for several years without writing a single note of the work.

He was highly self-critical, and perhaps this was to his disadvantage, for he discarded out of hand all those compositions he regarded as juvenilia, or with which he was not completely satisfied. We are therefore basically left with seven works which Furtwängler – as far as we know – sanctioned. First there was the *Te Deum* of 1909, which apparently goes back to sketches he made in the Medici Chapel in Florence as early as 1902. This work clearly has its roots in the nineteenth century. Nevertheless it had three performances between 1910 and 1911 and was impressive enough to convince that great *Kantor* at the *Thomaskirche* in Leipzig, Karl Straube, that it was 'worthy': he performed it in 1915. To the best of my knowledge this was the last performance of the *Te Deum* during Furtwängler's lifetime, but he wrote to Straube from Lübeck on 24 March 1915:

Peters [the music publishers] wrote to me some time ago, and I only answered them today. I did not send them, as they had wished, the score of my *Te Deum* immediately, as in view of my present experience I consider it necessary to revise the work completely in order to present it to the eyes of a publisher.

There is no evidence that he ever embarked on such a revision, and certainly the work has never appeared in print. In the same letter he writes:

If only I would finish the Quintet! The hope of having it performed in Leipzig is quite a spur.

We are led to believe that this refers to the Piano Quintet which was eventually completed in 1934/5. No matter what he may have projected in the intervening years, the fact remains that it was the first completed work for almost a quarter of a century. As far as one can gather, it never was performed at the time, except perhaps in private. The first known performances took place after his death. The work is in three movements, which last approximately 75 minutes. With all the admiration and respect I have for Furtwängler I find it difficult to listen with concentration to a piano quintet of such dimensions. True, the work is finely constructed, there are many moments of inspiration and beautiful romantic melodies but, in my humble opinion, it needs pruning.

The same apparently applies to the next completed composition which, unfortunately, I have never had the opportunity of hearing: the Violin Sonata No.1 in D minor. Early sketches date back to 1916, and the final score was completed in 1935. With this Sonata Furtwängler presented himself to the public as a composer for the first time since the last performance of the *Te Deum* (under Straube) in 1915. It must have surprised the audience to encounter Furtwängler in this guise, for the performances of so long before must have been forgotten by all but a few. In the event the première took place in Leipzig in March 1937 with Hugo Kolberg as soloist and Furtwängler himself at the piano. This Sonata was also the first of Furtwängler's compositions to appear in print.

Then came what is probably his most concise, his most compact composition, which he rightly entitled 'Symphonic

Concerto for Piano and Orchestra'. It is first mentioned in a letter to John Knittel, written in the Baltic holiday resort of Bansin on 27 July 1930 in reply to an invitation to visit Cairo:

> Your plan is lovely, it would be marvellous and something which I have wanted for a long time. But my work [Piano Concerto] which has already occupied me for several years *must* get finished this time.

Curiously enough, the composition was almost finished while he was holidaying with Knittel in Egypt, as is proved by a letter to Irme Schwab from Cairo on 7 March 1936. Of course he still revised and emended to the last, but it was first performed by himself with Edwin Fischer as soloist in Munich in 10 October 1937 and was perhaps the greatest success he had yet achieved as a composer. Granted, the work lasts about an hour, but there are no *longueurs*. It is compelling from beginning to end and – without making comparisons, which are invidious at any time – it seems to follow the same lines of thought that Brahms pursued in his two great concertos: all three have a powerful *obbligato* part for the pianist.

His next composition followed after only a short break: the Violin Sonata in D major in three movements, a much more concentrated work than the first Sonata. By now Furtwängler had his own unmistakable style, but there is something strange about this Second Sonata: according to the dating in the autograph copy, the last movement was completed on 12 September 1938, the second on 22 September, and the first on 28 September, so the entire work seems to have been written in a month, for no traces of earlier sketches can be found. Of course there may have been earlier sketches which have been lost or destroyed, but we can only judge on the basis of the available evidence. Furtwängler accompanied Georg Kulenkampff at the first performance which, according to Herzfeld (p.110), took place in February 1940.

For the rest of his working life Furtwängler was concerned only with symphonies. It is surprising how much he concentrated on composition during the 1930s and 40s. His work as a conductor continued, and he still needed as much time and energy in that direction as before, but it may well be that composing was a necessary antidote to the trials and

145

tribulations he constantly faced, and that in composing he could find inner peace, tranquillity and a refuge. However this may be, he was mainly engaged during the years 1938-41 – if we forget the early symphonic attempt of 1903 – on his Symphony No.1 in B minor. It is difficult to trace its history. In part it seems to go back to the 'Largo' or 'Symphonic Adagio in B minor' which he first conducted himself in Munich in 1906, but greatly altered. In addition there is an Adagio, a Scherzo, and a Finale, and there are two different versions of the Scherzo. We have a copy of the score by Wollheim. Apparently Furtwängler gave it a run-through at rehearsal – either completely or only two movements (authorities differ) – and was not satisfied. It is all most confusing. Perhaps he disavowed it and used some of the material for his second or third symphony. Yet he must have done some more work on it after 1945, for in a letter to Karl Straube on 14 July 1947 he writes:

> In autumn I shall present my Second Symphony of which I have just had the score and parts copied at my own expense. The First is also finished, and I am working to complete the Third. ... But I can't find a publisher. Schott (Strecker) [the Mainz publishers] have declined, because the music is not sufficiently up to date and modern.

The fact remains that, as far as we can discover, the work has never been heard except in that trial run-through.

There remain two last works to be discussed: Symphony No.2 in E minor and Symphony No.3 in C sharp minor. They occupied him during the last ten years of his life, for the earliest date we have for the Second is August 1944, and he was working on the Third up to 12 November 1954 before he went to the clinic at Ebersteinburg where he died on 30 November. The Second Symphony is on a grand Brucknerian scale in four movements and lasts about 75 minutes, of which the Finale alone takes about 24. It has its highly emotive moments. In parts it is great, but at times one wonders whether, with all its epic breadth and depth and its faultless symphonic conception and orchestration, it does not tend to be a little long, particularly in the Finale. He appears to have completed the work on 18 October 1945, for on that date he wrote to John Knittel:

> Today I have finished my Second Symphony and have locked it up safely, for the time being, in the safe of the clinic ['La Prairie'].

146

10. Furtwängler the Musician

As we have seen, he conducted it for the first time in Berlin on 22 February 1948 and many times afterwards – not only with the Berlin Philharmonic, but with other orchestras. On the whole it was always well received by the public and favourably reviewed in the press, but whether it was really the music which counted or the great love and respect in which Furtwängler was held as a personality and a conductor is difficult to estimate after the event.

There is little more to be said about the Third Symphony that has not been said already. Together with the Piano Concerto it is my favourite composition of Furtwängler. It is deeply moving, a magnificent hulk in its three movements: *Largo*, *Allegro*, *Adagio*. The sequential repetitions he was so fond of now take on a structural meaning and are no longer tedious *Schusterflecken* – 'cobbler's patches'. The titles he himself gave to the first three movements (see above) are ample evidence that he knew he was not far from death, and Bruckner's description of the Adagio of his Ninth could equally well apply to this unfinished symphony: *Abschied vom Leben* – 'Farewell to Life'. The work is permeated by an ineffable sadness. It reflects the fact that Furtwängler was a tragic figure, almost a character in a Greek or Shakespearian tragedy, and this is indeed his Swan Song.

People like to 'classify' composers. If that is necessary, we could say that Furtwängler follows in the footsteps of Max von Schillings (1868-1939), Hans Pfitzner (1869-1949), Max Reger (1873-1916). Richard Strauss is said to have described himself as 'a first-class second-rate composer'. This dictum might justifiably be applied to Furtwängler. Will his works ever gain a place in the regular concert repertoire? Only time will tell.

How then do we assess his output as a composer? I have said before that Furtwängler was honest and sincere in his attitude to music and an utter craftsman as a composer. As a nineteenth-century musician he may have had his roots in Brahms, Bruckner, Wagner and, to a lesser extent, Richard Strauss. But he was no mere epigone: every great composer has his roots in the past. Like all the others, he thrived on the past and gave these reminiscences his own personal stamp. But although he derives from the romantic composers, it was Beethoven he looked up to as the greatest of them all, especially

147

in the matter of form. Fortunately we have the evidence, and in his own voice, in one of the few extant recordings of Furtwängler addressing a colloquium of students in 1950, where he expounds his formal ideas:

> A symphonic production presupposes an idea which, from the very beginning, cannot be realised in any other way except symphonically and except on this large canvas. A symphonic work must have two, three, four themes which share a common experience, promote each other's growth and assist each other towards a goal, similar perhaps to the way in which individual characters in a Shakespeare drama influence each other's destinies. When the so-called recapitulation comes it must be something completely different, on a completely different plane from the beginning, because so much has happened already, and the resultant effect of the entire work has its origin in the correlation of these themes. One single theme cannot achieve this, but only the polarity between the themes.

What is often ignored is that Furtwängler was an all-round musician, such as Hindemith – himself one of the great all-round musicians of our century – extolled in *A Composer's World* (Cambridge, Mass. 1952). Apart from composing and conducting, Furtwängler also was a first-class pianist. Indeed in his Breslau days he was especially admired as a repetiteur, for he could play the most difficult conductor's or vocal scores at sight. He maintained this ability. It is recorded that, in his youth, the pocket scores of the seventeen Beethoven String Quartets were his constant companion on his travels, and throughout his life he was apparently able to sit down at the piano and play any movement of any of them from memory. He also played concertos by Bach (especially the triple concerto) and Mozart, directing from the piano, but unfortunately we only have three items of recorded evidence of his piano skill. Two are recordings of Furtwängler himself playing the keyboard part in Bach's Brandenburg Concerto No.5. The other is the recital of Hugo Wolf songs when he accompanied Elisabeth Schwarzkopf in Salzburg on 12 August 1953. On 19 December 1952 Schwarzkopf was Furtwängler's soprano soloist in Turin in Beethoven's Ninth. Walter Legge in his sleeve note to the Salzburg Wolf recording, issued later, comments:

> Over supper after the concert he [Furtwängler] said, with the

school-boyish diffidence which was one of the most attractive features of his personality: 'I hear you are giving a Wolf recital at the next Salzburg Festival. If you haven't already engaged a pianist, may I be considered?' Schwarzkopf accepted immediately and incredulously. This was more than any singer dared hope to expect.

That year, Furtwängler stayed in Aigen outside Salzburg. Schwarzkopf, who was living in the neighbourhood, often passed his house and heard him practising first scales, then the pianistically more difficult songs in the programme with all the concentration of a student before his finals.

We can count ourselves happy that a recording of this recital has been preserved.

In this context it is worth noting that Furtwängler was a magnificent accompanist, not only as a pianist, but as a conductor. This has often been attributed to his initial training in opera, both as a repetiteur and as a conductor, in Breslau, Zürich, Munich, Strasbourg. That may be, but it is also true that most other conductors in Germany had a similar background, and not all of them were such perfect accompanists. In the case of Furtwängler there are two antithetical reasons which gave him the gift to accompany as he did. One was that he had the ability to feel with his soloists, to breathe – or bow – with them, as the case might be, and to put himself in their place. On the other hand he was an autocrat who imposed his own musical will on his soloists and, in a way, *conducted* them instead of *following* them. There were a few who resented this, but the majority appreciated his guidance which, as has been mentioned before, enabled them to grow beyond their stature. In 1952, in Salzburg, Furtwängler rehearsed Mozart's *Figaro*, but before the first performance he was taken seriously ill and could not conduct any of the performances. Schwarzkopf remembered the occasion, and in the BBC Documentary of 30 November 1964 she commented:

> The slow arias were really very, very slow. ... Furtwängler's slow tempi were always comfortable and he carried you on a cushion all the time. ... Then another conductor had to take over. He tried to take the same tempi and it was impossible: it was only he [Furtwängler] who could really sustain these tempi.

On the other hand Furtwängler was no teacher. He never took private pupils. Nor did he ever participate in 'Master Classes for

Conductors' so dearly beloved in our day. He made his view quite clear in a letter addressed to Igor Markewitsch on 17 September 1953:

> I am very honoured by your invitation to participate in your Master Class and regret not to be able to accept. I am not of the opinion that one can learn and teach conducting in isolation from the works which are to be interpreted. Conducting is something which can be taught and rationalised very easily if one only tackles it from the easy and rational aspect. But it becomes extraordinarily difficult when it comes to fathoming the depths of great works. After all, the conducting technique is the same as other techniques and, in the end, only demands a technical interest. Much more important ... it would be to try to restore order in the productive outlook which we have on music in our day and age, and which is completely depraved and in ruins.

That does not mean that he was uninterested in education. He lectured and wrote articles on Beethoven, Brahms, Bruckner and Wagner, and on various aspects of musical life. And he was always kind and helpful to young musicians who came to him with a specific question. Here I can tell a personal story.

During the interval of a rehearsal in March 1953 I came to him with a question. It concerned a tempo relationship in Brahms's 'Tragic Overture'. I told him my worries, and he said to me quite simply: 'My dear young friend, why don't you allow your heart to speak? Whenever you conduct, whenever you make music, always follow the dictates of your heart. That does not mean that the brain can go to sleep. The intellect must always remain awake – but it is only there to control the heart, to make sure that the heart does not go to excess.' In those few words, after studying with many others, I received the greatest music lesson of my life.

Nikisch must have had a somewhat similar attitude. I was on good terms with Sir Adrian Boult and once, over lunch, I asked him whether it was correct that in Leipzig he had been a pupil of Nikisch. He replied: 'Actually, no, because Nikisch never had private pupils. I knew him, he was most kind and helpful to me, and he allowed me to attend all his rehearsals. In those rehearsals – more than in his concerts – I learnt enormously from him. So you can call me his disciple, but not his student.'

*

10. Furtwängler the Musician

We must now consider what is probably the most important topic for most readers: Furtwängler the conductor. Much has been written, and is being written, on that subject and, unhappily, with the passage of time the number of those who can write about it from personal knowledge is growing smaller and smaller. Most know Furtwängler only from gramophone records, and I may be putting the cart before the horse. All media of mechanical reproduction were anathema to Furtwängler, for to him the *Gemeinschaftserlebnis,* 'the communal experience' of conductor, orchestra *and* audience in the spirit of the composer, was supreme. He could not feel at home in a recording studio where there was no human response. This was not only in the days of 78s when everything had to be chopped up into sides of four or four and a half minutes, but also later when longer stretches could be recorded on tape but the flow of the music was being interrupted by producers and editors. A case in point was his recording of Schumann's Symphony No.4 for *Deutsche Grammophon* in Berlin in May 1953. The producer interrupted him again and again, asking for re-takes. In the end Furtwängler lost his temper, insisted that all previous takes should be scrapped and that he would now play Schumann IV from beginning to end. They were at liberty to record it, and they were free to issue that performance if they felt like it, but there were to be no edits whatsoever. The performance was recorded, it was issued, and it is one of the greatest Furtwängler recordings in existence. But apart from this isolated instance, the greatest Furtwängler recordings we possess are those which were recorded at live concerts, for then he was really at one with himself and his audience. The only exception to this precept I can quote is his recording of Wagner's *Tristan* of 1952. When he heard the test pressing for the second time he began to see that, with modern techniques, there might be something in mechanical reproduction after all – but by then it was too late.

In connection with this *Tristan* recording it is important to note again Furtwängler's fairness and impartiality. We have already heard that during the recording sessions he had irrevocably fallen out with Walter Legge, and that Legge was a man he hated – perhaps the only person who attracted his undying personal hatred. Yet Furtwängler could always keep personal sentiments and professional appreciation apart, and in her memoirs of Walter Legge Elisabeth Schwarzkopf writes that after hearing the test pressings 'Furtwängler told Walter that his name should also be on the label since it was truly a joint effort'. Legge added: 'It was the only praise I ever received from the great conductor.'

*

When we try to assess a conductor from the inside, it is not enough to listen to performances and records: the true character becomes apparent in his rehearsals. Furtwängler always studied his scores as if he had never seen them before. In the same way he expected his orchestra to give a 'first performance' each time. He was the sworn enemy of routine, and in a BBC broadcast of 1948 he once expressed it as follows:

> The conductor has one arch-enemy to fight: routine. Routine is very human, very understandable, it is the line of least resistance and there is no denying that in daily life it has its advantages. But all the more must we insist that it plays the most deadly role in music, especially in the performance of old and familiar works. In fact routine with its loveless mediocrity and its treacherous perfection lies like hoar-frost on the performance of the most beautiful and best known works.

In this fight against routine he always retained his freshness of outlook to the very end, just as he always maintained his belief in improvisation – but more of this later.

His manner of rehearsing was unorthodox, to say the least. He played long stretches of a work without saying anything, and when he did stop his usual words were 'No, no, once again'. At most he added 'This time with me', pointing to his baton. He was not fussy and relied on his players to notice minor technical deficiencies themselves. Though he usually had orchestras of a calibre in which he could place such trust, his basic principle was to treat his players as equal artists. They made music together almost in the way that chamber musicians work together, with himself as *primus inter pares*. Thereby he made them greater than they actually were, as he did his soloists. How different from a conductor I once heard rehearse Beethoven's *Eroica*. He spent a full three-hour rehearsal on the exposition of the first movement, rehearsing bar by bar. When it came to the performance we had hundreds of perfect individual bars, but the movement did not coalesce. With Furtwängler it was always the line, the phrase, that mattered, and small technical details were of relatively minor importance. In any case his instructions were usually very vague, as is exemplified by Piatigorsky in his memoirs:

> Furtwängler, after pleading with the orchestra, 'Gentleman, this phrase must be – it must – it must – you know what I mean – please try again – please', said to me at the intermission, 'You see how important it is for a conductor to convey his wishes clearly?' Strangely, the orchestra knew what he wanted.

On the other hand, when he did speak at length he was always cogent and referred to the structure, the line, the phrase. There were two occasions on which I was present which exemplify the point.

One was when he was rehearsing the Beethoven Violin Concerto. We all know that it starts with five timpani beats and on the fifth the main theme begins. Furtwängler stopped the orchestra and said: 'No, gentlemen, the timpani may have stopped, but you must carry it on in your inner ear, because it remains an organ point for the next bars.' The other occasion was when he rehearsed the beginning of Mozart's G minor Symphony. He told the violins: 'The first bars are only repeated Ds – the quaver E flats are merely grace notes.' This just shows how Furtwängler always thought symphonically – in contrast to Toscanini, who thought operatically. This is not to denigrate Toscanini, but to point out the basic dissimilarity in the attitude of these two great conductors.

The question has often been asked which of the two orchestras with whom Furtwängler was most closely associated was his favourite, the Berlin or the Vienna. He answered the question himself in an interview in October 1950 with a Danish music critic of the *Berlingske Tidende*:

> My relationship to these two exceptional orchestras is, I imagine, akin to that of a man with two wives. He doesn't know which he prefers. One of them has blue eyes, the other brown – but they are equally pretty, and he loves them both. How should I be able to classify such eminent artistic capacities?

When it comes to interpretation, we are on delicate grounds. First and foremost it must be said that he always knew his scores by heart, even when he did not conduct from memory. The other point is the supreme feeling of responsibility he felt towards the composer, even though at times there may have been works which he did not particularly like. As Birkner put it in his foreword to *Aufzeichnungen* (p.8):

> He was completely aware of his own greatness, but the awareness of his greatness made him humble in face of the responsibility which had thereby been laid on him.

That this applied to Beethoven, Brahms, Bruckner and the like goes without saying, but it applied equally to contemporary composers. Frau Schoenberg recalls:

> After a rehearsal, through the duration of the dinner and until we left, the conversation was simply how he should conduct a piece [Variations for Orchestra, Op.31], he wanted to do it in the intention of the composer ...

On another occasion, in April 1954, after he had conducted a performance of Blacher's *Concertante Musik*, he rang the composer late at night to find out what had gone wrong. Blacher had not come to the artists' room afterwards because Furtwängler was besieged by his fans. Blacher was quite disconcerted to be telephoned and said that it was the first time a conductor had bothered to enquire whether the performance had been as he had envisaged it. Furtwängler replied: 'Well, that is probably because I am a composer myself, and I know only too well what it means to expose oneself in public.'

But of course it is in the master-works of the classic and romantic periods that Furtwängler's interpretations were at their greatest, and here we cannot go by recordings. Furtwängler was, as I have said, a tragic figure, and it was in those works of a deeply tragic character that he was at his finest: Mozart's G minor, Beethoven's Fifth, Bruckner's Ninth, Brahms's Third, Tchaikovsky's *Pathétique*. Here he was alone. Here he came face to face with his destiny, his God.

Furtwängler's interpretations and tempi have been the

subject of much criticism. True, he continually improvised, and on more than one occasion he said himself that at the performance there must be no more improvisation than at the rehearsal, *but no less either*. He knew his scores to the last detail, and the straightforward concept was an iron framework for him – but within this framework he left himself free to respond to the spur of the moment. He had the unlimited ability to submit to his inspiration without breaking the bounds of the given structure. His tempo, carefully adjusted to the acoustics of whatever hall he was performing in, was ever flexible. As Eugen Jochum put it:

> When he modified the tempo, he modified it so wonderfully that the listener did not feel that it was a modification.

Similarly Szymon Goldberg, leader of the Berlin Philharmonic from 1929-34, remarked:

> He knew exactly what he did. His way of music-making created the impression that he would permanently improvise, but it really was not so. He conducted according to a very definite plan, and what was generally supposed to be improvisation was just imaginative planning.

In the words of Hans Keller, what he basically needed as an interpreter was enough space for phrase and drama. Space tends towards slowness, drama towards quickness.

This is why people believe he tended towards slow tempi. The ambiguous answer is: he did and he did not. He knew precisely in what passages, whether in opera or in a symphonic work, he could spread himself, and which passages he had to move along. Despite all preconceived notions, he is on record as having conducted Beethoven's Ninth at Bayreuth in the shortest space of time, and at *La Scala*, for the first act of *Parsifal*, he took 103 minutes, as opposed to Toscanini (120 minutes) and the 'fast' Richard Strauss (110 minutes).

We must now consider his attitude to the concept of *Werktreue* – 'authenticity' or 'faithfulness to the work' – which can be interpreted variously. Basically he followed his great predecessor Arthur Nikisch, who thought it more important to bring out the *essence* of the work than make it sound exactly the same as in bygone days. In fact he wrote a long article in a

Leipzig newspaper ending with the words: 'I simply cannot bring myself to pay homage to the accumulated layers of dust in libraries.' Nowadays it has become fashionable to be 'authentic' by employing period instruments and the same number of musicians, but this is simply a matter of orthography, especially if other considerations are ignored, such as playing a Brandenburg Concerto, envisaged for a small *salon* at Court, in the vast surroundings of the Royal Albert Hall. This was not for Furtwängler. He did not stick to the technicalities, but regarded 'authenticity' as being faithful to the spirit of the composer by trying to communicate to the ears of a twentieth-century audience, accustomed to the acoustics of modern concert halls and vast symphony orchestras, what the composer meant to say in his time. It may shock today's purists that Furtwängler played Bach's Third Brandenburg with the full complement of about 60 strings, and that he himself played the piano part in the Fifth on a modern concert grand in a completely 'unauthentic' style. But in his performances the whole spirituality, the whole deep meaning, of Bach came across. After all, we have no means of knowing how Bach himself would have reacted if he had had similar forces at his disposal, if he had had a Bechstein or Steinway grand, if he could have made use of the silvery tone of a Böhm flute instead of the recorders of his age. Szymon Goldberg had a similar approach when he said that 'people think that if they are not bored by the music of Bach it has not been played in the right style!'

One question has been ignored so far: Furtwängler's repertoire. Furtwängler is always considered as the great interpreter of the classics and romantics. True, and his programmes bear it out; but what is not true is that he ignored contemporary music. Unfortunately the information at our disposal is somewhat incomplete, and I shall therefore base my comments on the evidence of Herzfeld (who compiles long lists going up to 1940) and Henning Smidth Olsen's detailed compilation of the concert programmes from 1947 to his death in 1954. Unfortunately there is a gap between 1941 and 1945, for which I have been able to trace very little documentation. The basic trend, however, should become clear if we consider the pre-1940 and the post-1947 periods separately.

10. Furtwängler the Musician

Because it was published under the Nazi regime, Herzfeld's lists comprising the years 1911-40 completely ignore compositions by Mendelssohn, Mahler and other 'undesirable' composers. What remains relevant is that during that period Furtwängler conducted a total of 1045 performances of works by Beethoven, 519 by Brahms, 153 by Bruckner, 173 by Mozart, 200 by Haydn, 171 by Schubert, 164 by Schumann, 320 by Richard Strauss, 132 by Tchaikovsky and 319 by Wagner (this is only in concert and excludes opera performances). The work he conducted most frequently was Beethoven's Fifth (148 times), and the only works in the repertoire in which he exceeded his 'century' were Beethoven VII (130 times), Brahms I (117 times), *Till Eulenspiegel* (120 times) and the *Meistersinger* Prelude (116 times). He also conducted in that period a total of 328 performances of works by 129 contemporary composers. Of course two points must be taken into consideration. One is that many of the works that may have been contemporary in, say, 1925 are now part of our standard concert repertoire. Secondly, when we look through Herzfeld's list we see the names of many composers who, at best, awaken a mere flicker of memory.

From 1947 onwards the picture changes somewhat. Beethoven still remains pre-eminent with a total of 273 performances of his symphonies of which, of course, the Fifth predominates with 63 performances. The Brahms symphonies come a close second, with 120 performances, and the Haydn Variations with 24. Strangely enough, the Richard Strauss Tone Poems also take an important place, especially *Till Eulenspiegel* with 44 peformances and *Tod und Verklärung* with 27. But when it comes to contemporary music he played relatively little. In his post-war programmes Ravel (if he can still be called contemporary) is represented by 31 performances, Debussy by 22 and Hindemith by 17. This may seem incongruous since Furtwängler considered himself a composer and saw it as his duty to further the cause of his colleagues. But he was compelled to take this course by concert entrepreneurs: such was his international reputation as an interpreter of the great German repertoire of the nineteenth century that they would not let him conduct anything else. In a letter to Ernest Ansermet of 28 July 1947 he wrote:

157

In Salzburg my second concert will also be with Menuhin. I suggested the Bartok Concerto which would have interested me very much, but I was asked to do the Brahms. That is the position: I must only conduct Brahms and Beethoven, and you only Stravinsky and Bartok!!!

Finally, the unanswered and unanswerable question remains: wherein lay Furtwängler's supreme greatness as a conductor and interpreter? I hate to come up with clichés like charisma, personality, power of conviction, but how is one to define the indefinable? Perhaps I shall come nearest the mark if I tell of a personal experience. A close friend of mine, the late Deryck Cooke, and I once went together to the Royal Albert Hall to hear Furtwängler. The programme included Schumann's Fourth. At the end the whole audience was on its feet, including Deryck and me, applauding wildly. Deryck was shouting 'Bravo, bravo, bravo!' Then he leant over to me and said: 'You can't play Schumann that way – bravo, bravo! – He's pulled the thing to pieces completely – bravo, bravo, bravo!' Such was the mesmeric influence of Furtwängler, and as he took his bow in his shy and diffident manner he reminded me of those famous words supposedly said by Martin Luther on 18 April 1521 at the Diet of Worms:

Here I stand. I can no other.
God help me. Amen.

Furtwängler: a tribute

by Neville Cardus

The following was written by Neville Cardus as an introduction to the printed programme of a concert given on 30 November 1964 (the tenth anniversary of Furtwängler's death) by the Royal Philharmonic Orchestra in the Royal Albert Hall, London, conducted by Hans-Hubert Schönzeler.

Furtwängler was a conductor fairly to be called creative. He himself said of his early experimental years that he had to rethink his view of the masterpieces. 'I repudiated every schematic pattern of interpretation, every so-called tradition, which enables many conductors to evade personal inter-pretation.'

He was a conductor at the extreme of the 'objective' school that believes music 'should be left to speak for itself'. His frequent underlinings, his sometimes excessive overstatements (and understatements) were the consequence of a vision searching always. He had no use for the 'objective' score – the truth is not as easily demonstrated as all that. The score for Furtwängler was the ground-plan, the blue-print, from which imagination, guided by great knowledge, got to work. 'I cannot,' he said, 'adjust myself and transform myself as easily as a man who is *only* a conductor.' He would have agreed with Mahler's saying – 'Not all the music is in the printed notes.'

He wasn't a music-maker for all tastes. He made fanatical followers and also repelled the tastes of many others. Critics in London, notably Ernest Newman, fell foul of Furtwängler's personal reactions; these critics were propagandists of the theory that a score is an object plainly to be seen and heard as in itself it really is. Furtwängler, being German, could readily, had he thought it worth while, have produced metaphysical arguments to show how difficult it is to chase 'objective truth', except by means of the variable senses of the subjective self. To the critic who protested that a Furtwängler pianissimo was 'exaggerated' he might have retorted, 'Are you sure that your ears were objectively positioned; was your seat in the hall the throne of demonstrable truth?'

Music for Furtwängler was the main way of his life. To describe him as a 'romantic' is superficial. He mingled feeling and a large comprehensive view of structure. He was serious in mind and, in the presence of music, austere at times. Not often did he give a smile to music. Yet nobody has excelled the gigantic stride, swing and bucolic humours of Furtwängler's treatment of the Seventh and Eighth symphonies of Beethoven. But it was a humour above life-size, laughter of the belly of the universe.

His unfolding of the Ninth symphony of Beethoven was, in my opinion, the biggest-scaled, most inward thinking in the slow movement, and cosmic in the first, that I have ever heard. The *adagio* began with the tone descent of the dove, so to say. His conducting of *Tristan und Isolde* was matchless in intensity and control of encompassing outlines. The pauses he risked in the beginning of the Prelude caused me once, when attending a rehearsal, to think that something had gone wrong in the submerged orchestral pit. But, as soon as the orchestra was heard again at the end of bar 5 we could all realise that in the silences, and all subsequent silences, the heart of the music continued to beat. A silence by Furtwängler wasn't just a cessation of sound; it was a living pulse beating.

He was a tall man, with a high dome of a forehead, withdrawn of aspect on the platform, until he set the music in motion. He would bow just once to the audience. Then he attacked a symphony with a convulsion of the neck threatening to dislodge his head. And his baton gyrated corkscrew, apparently combining up- and down-beats simultaneously. A renowned critic wrote that from his seat in the hall he was quite unable to 'follow Furtwängler's beat'. I couldn't resist pointing out in my own paper that, so long as the Berlin Philharmonic Orchestra could follow Furtwängler's beat, it hardly mattered that my distinguished and learned colleague couldn't.

A violinist in the Berlin Philharmonic asked me to make a long special journey to hear Furtwängler conducting the *Pathétique* symphony of Tchaikovsky. I protested: 'A long journey just to hear the *Pathétique*? I can hear a good performance of it any day.' My Berlin violinist simply repeated, 'Come and hear Furtwängler's performance.' It was the most powerfully tragic, tormented and emotionally shaking, yet most clinchingly shaped performance of the work that I have ever heard, or ever can hope to hear. Moreover, the terror and self-flagellations in the music, the charnelhouse descents, were somehow ennobled by Furtwängler's humane treatment of every nuance.

He attended as scrupulously to the written notes as any purist. But he tried to find out, by his emphasis on this or that tonal factor, what the underlying conception was when the work was actually being born in the composer's mind. Furtwängler could never fall into a routine of efficient standardised performance. For him a rehearsal was not an affair of putting on orchestral polish; it was a means of increasing the pregnancy. 'The essentials of a performance,' he maintained, 'cannot be determined in advance.' He seemed, as he conducted, to be a lonely searching Faustian figure, never complacent, absolutely intent on the 'inside' of a work; but not submerged in it so much that he could not watch every step. In the mind of the creative conductor (and actor) a watch must always be kept on what is being technically done. A climax by Furtwängler was sometimes heaven-scaling. But he himself remained secure, anchored. He had extraordinary intuitions. If a passage of a score eluded his understanding he would follow the persuasions of his heart.

I have frequently imagined, hearing a Furtwängler performance, that he could be thought of not only as conducting, but actually composing the music, as it moved along and onward. The truth is that Furtwängler was himself a composer – frustrated. Among his compositions are two large-scaled symphonies, and a sonata for violin and piano in four movements which goes on for round about an hour. His second symphony is finely and resonantly scored, remembering his beloved masters, notably Bruckner. It is to be hoped that the BBC will give us a chance in this country of hearing his second symphony. His interpretations occasionally seemed to suggest that in the masterpieces of Beethoven, Bruckner and the rest he was endeavouring to find a channel for his own aspirations as a composer, seeking liberation for his own conceptions by collaboration with fulfilled musical genius.

He had a sensitive ear for orchestral tone, both for the character of each instrument and for tone in the mass. Though he could treat a melody with any amount of suavity, eloquence and flow, he at the same time attended, perhaps more than any other conductor, to strength, depth and potency of harmony. Most conductors appear to begin from the main 'top-line' themes and work downward. Music with Furtwängler took its rise from the fundamental tone. Under his direction the lower strings of the Berlin Philharmonic became unrivalled for fulness and flexibility. In music he realised the whole man of himself. If ever a conductor was a dedicated artist Furtwängler stood foremost in his period. The last time I saw him was at a Lucerne music festival, not many months before his death. He was in the audience listening to Brahms played by Fischer, Schneiderhan and Mainardi. He looked pale and tired as the music began; then it was as if the sight and sense of the visible mortal universe left him, as he entered the only world that truly brought to him ease and freedom of spirit. He was, as I say, a dedicated musician. Not all conductors are that.

Recommended Reading

Books by and about Wilhelm Furtwängler are legion, but most of them are in German only. Very few have been translated into English, and the number of original publications in English is small.

Most essential, of course, are his own writings. He stubbornly refused to write an autobiography, as he considered that personal details were of no importance and that his views as a musician were all that mattered. The most important publication under his own name is therefore his *Gespräche über Musik* (Zürich 1948, Engl. transl. *Concerning Music*, London 1953).[1] This consists of seven conversations with Walter Abendroth in 1937. Furtwängler and Abendroth talked on predetermined musical subjects; the talks were taken down and subsequently edited. Later Furtwängler added an epilogue about his views on contemporary music. All in all, this book represents Furtwängler's musical *Credo*.

Throughout his life he carried a notebook with him and, whether sitting in trains or hotel rooms after a concert, he jotted down his thoughts. Typically, these concerned only music, philosophy or art in general, never personal emotions. Nevertheless during his lifetime he authorised a volume called *Ton und Wort: Aufsätze und Vorträge 1918-1954* (Wiesbaden 1954), a collection of letters, lectures and thoughts about German music and art, including contentious subjects that

---

[1] All places and dates given refer to the first edition, but most of these works have been reprinted subsequently.

163

arose in the Nazi period. (In his *Furtwängler Recalled* – see below – Daniel Gillis says that this book appeared in an English translation in London in 1965 under the title 'Collected Essays'. The project was indeed planned, but it never came to fruition.) After his death all his diaries and notebooks and most of his letters went into the keeping of his widow, Frau Elisabeth Furtwängler, and eventually three important collections appeared. First there was *Vermächtnis: Nachgelassene Schriften* (Wiesbaden 1956), a collection of notebook jottings followed by essays and fragmentary writings. Then came a volume of letters (Wiesbaden 1964), selected and edited by Franz Thiess. It is not a complete edition of Furtwängler's letters, since many are in private hands and others were withheld for personal reasons. Lastly, we have *Wilhelm Furtwängler, Aufzeichnungen 1924-1954* (Wiesbaden 1980; Engl. transl. *Wilhelm Furtwängler, Notebooks 1924-1954*, London & New York 1989). This is a selection and collation of diary notes prepared by Elisabeth Furtwängler and Günter Birkner. If we read these notes in chronological order we get as good an understanding as we can of Furtwängler's spiritual development. Finally, there is a slim volume in the Reclam Collection (Stuttgart 1952) containing three previously published essays on Brahms and Bruckner with an epilogue by Walter Riezler summing up what Furtwängler meant to him as a man and a musician.

The first biography proper was written in 1940, by Friedrich Herzfeld, *Wilhelm Furtwängler: Weg und Wesen* (Leipzig 1941), which has never been translated into English. It is excellent as far as it goes, and is useful for the detailed lists of Furtwängler's repertoire. But it was written under the Nazis and, since Herzfeld was partly Jewish, he had to be doubly careful with everything he wrote. So we find no mention of composers like Mahler and Mendelssohn, and when Furtwängler's appointment in Mannheim in 1915 is discussed it is merely said that he owed much to the recommendation of 'the then Munich *Generalmusikdirektor*', without any mention that this was Bruno Walter. According to Grove, it was reissued in 1950 in a revised version. Presumably this was a 'denazified' version, but I have not been able to get hold of it myself. By all accounts

Furtwängler himself never read the book.

Then we have Curt Riess, *Wilhelm Furtwängler: Musik und Politik* (Berne 1953; Engl. transl. *Wilhelm Furtwängler*, London 1955). The details of how this book came about have already been told. Furtwängler knew Riess, read the book and expressed himself in a disapproving letter to him on 25 September 1953:

> I fully realise that you have written the book with the best of intentions and in order to do me justice, and those who nowadays are still interested in political happenings will certainly get their money's worth. ... I am an artist who is in the middle of life and in a state of development, but about whose actual position your book does not say a single word. The reason is that no non-musician can write a biography about a musician of my type ...

In this matter Furtwängler was distinctly unjust, even though, like many journalists, Riess was somewhat slipshod in biographical details. Riess was essentially right. The sub-title of his book was 'Music and Politics', and in this context it cannot be judged as simple biography.

Karla Höcker, who has probably written more about Furtwängler than anyone, was originally a viola player but later turned to journalism. In 1942 she was invited by the Berlin Philharmonic to accompany them on their tour of Sweden to write articles and give her personal impressions. This led to a personal friendship with the Furtwänglers – a friendship, incidentally, which still exists with Frau Elisabeth. Her first publication was a slim volume entitled *Sinfonische Reise* (Gütersloh 1954) which, unfortunately, like many of her books, is now out of print; none as far as I know has ever been translated into English. She followed this up with *Wilhelm Furtwängler: Begegnungen und Gespräche* (Berlin 1961) and *Die nie vergessenen Klänge: Erinnerungen an Wilhelm Furtwängler* (Berlin 1979). Both books are somewhat similar in character, in that they report personal experiences she had with Furtwängler on tour with the orchestra and little anecdotes; but they also contain conversations in greater depth on various musical subjects on other occasions. Finally, her most important book is *Wilhelm Furtwängler: Dokumente, Berichte, Bilder und Aufzeichnungen* (Berlin 1968). This is what the title implies: a collection of documents, pictorial material and biographical details.

As will have become clear, most of the writings about Furtwängler were published after his death. Perhaps the earliest publication was a booklet in the series 'The Great Interpreters' published by R. Kister of Geneva. The series is mainly pictorial, with photographs by Roger Hauert accompanied by a brief text. *Furtwängler* appeared in 1955, though most of Hauert's photos seem to date from about 1953. The text by Bernard Gavoty, the leading music critic of *Le Figaro*, is succinct but acute. The series exists in German, French and English versions. The first important book about Furtwängler, however, was one edited by Martin Hürlimann: *Wilhelm Furtwängler im Urteil seiner Zeit* (Zürich 1955). This contains *in memoriam* tributes from prominent artists, as well as accounts of various periods in Furtwängler's career and of his connections with different centres such as Berlin, Vienna, Salzburg, Lucerne and Paris. One of the most interesting articles is by Hürlimann himself: 'Furtwängler in Switzerland'. However, the book which probably has the greatest immediacy and authenticity was written by his widow Elisabeth Furtwängler: *Über Wilhelm Furtwängler* (Wiesbaden 1979). Apart from his parents, his brother and his sisters, now all dead, there is probably no one who knew Furtwängler as well as she did, and no one to whom he was so utterly devoted. The whole book breathes the spirit of this intimacy.

In 1965 appeared what was probably the first book on Furtwängler published originally in English – Daniel Gillis's *Furtwängler Recalled* (Zürich & New York 1965). Gillis is a Professor of Latin and Greek at Haverford College and an ardent music lover. Modelled on *Wilhelm Furtwängler im Urteil seiner Zeit*, it includes articles from that book, supplemented by many new contributions. To explain what the book is about we may best quote from his own introduction:

> The following pages come from the pens of three generations of writers – conductors, opera singers, composers, pianists, concert masters, cellists, violinists, correspondents, critics who knew Furtwängler only on the podium, and orchestral musicians who played under him for decades. These writers have tried to express what Furtwängler was, what he meant, and what he gave them. ...

Gillis followed this book up with another, *Furtwängler and America* (New York 1970). This is perhaps the best researched publication on the unpleasant subject of Furtwängler's relations with the New World and covers his three guest visits (1925/26/27), the troubles with the New York Philharmonic-Symphony Orchestra (1937), his 'denazification' (1946) and all the nastiness connected with the Chicago affair (1948). It is altogether a most courageous book.

Furtwängler and Great Britain by John Squire & John Hunt (London 1985) gives a detailed account of all Furtwängler's concert and opera performances in Great Britain up to his death, with many facsimiles, complete programme details, and many excerpts from interviews and press notices. The second half of the paperback volume includes a revised edition of *The Furtwängler Sound* by John Hunt, the Chairman of the Wilhelm Furtwängler Society (UK), which will be dealt with later.

The 100th anniversary of Furtwängler's birth brought a spate of books. The most important was Fred K. Prieberg, *Kraftprobe: Wilhelm Furtwängler im Dritten Reich* (Wiesbaden 1986), neither a biography nor a discussion of the musician, but a carefully researched documentation with meticulous references to all the available evidence about Furtwängler's political position during the years 1933-45. It makes difficult reading, even for someone fluent in German, but as a source of documentary evidence it is indispensable. There have been various books about the 'mystique' of Furtwängler's conducting but, as has been said before, these do not really lead us anywhere. Two perhaps are worth mentioning: one is a slender volume by Arnd-Volker Listewnik and Hedwig Sander, *Wilhelm Furtwängler* (Leipzig 1986), which though it does not contribute anything very new contains a detailed account of Furtwängler's years at the *Gewandhaus* and several facsimiles of letters and newspaper articles. Lastly, there is a recent publication, edited by Gottfried Kraus, *Ein Mass, das heute fehlt: Wilhelm Furtwängler im Echo der Nachwelt* (Salzburg 1986). In principle it is a rehash of both Hürlimann's *Furtwängler im Urteil seiner Zeit* and Gillis's *Furtwängler Recalled* with some new contributions, but mainly it is intended for German readers who cannot read English or French. There has also been a book in

French, *Furtwängler: une biographie par le disque* by Gérard Gefen (Paris 1986). This concentrates on the discography and will principally interest the record collector, but it also contains a certain amount of biographical material juxtaposed in a chronology with other events. Most recently two other books have appeared (in German) which have a distinct bearing on Furtwängler. One is by Werner Thärichen, who was for many years the principal timpanist of the Berlin Philharmonic, entitled *Paukenschläge: Furtwängler oder Karajan* (Zürich/ Berlin 1987). The other is by Klaus Lang, *Lieber Herr Celibidache ...* (Zürich/St Gallen 1988), which highlights the whole situation of the Berlin Philharmonic after 1945.

There remains one other group of publications: those dealing simply and factually with Furtwängler's programmes and recordings. The first to appear was a collation by Peter Wackernagel, *Wilhelm Furtwängler: Die Programme der Konzerte mit dem Berliner Philharmonsichen Orchester 1922-1954* (Wiesbaden 1965) which lists all programmes (including some special concerts) conducted by Furtwängler in Berlin in the orchestra's subscription series during those years. Similarly, Henning Smidth Olsen compiled his *Konzertprogramme, Opern und Vorträge 1947 bis 1954* (Wiesbaden 1972), but he excluded all studio sessions. Of the greatest importance is the same author's *Wilhelm Furtwängler: A Discography* (Copenhagen 1970) and the second revised and updated edition (North American Wilhelm Furtwängler Society 1973). Obviously these are now outdated, as so much new material has been found, but there seems to be little hope of a third edition. Finally there is a most valiant effort by John Hunt who brought out a booklet called *The Furtwängler Sound* (London 1982). Being both a Furtwängler enthusiast and having a specialist knowledge of recordings in general, his listing proves invaluable, as does his second and revised edition of 1985, which comprises the second half of *Furtwängler and Great Britain* cited earlier. Hunt lists all known and extant recordings of Furtwängler under composers in alphabetical order and thereby complements Henning Smidth Olsen's chronological discography. It is to be hoped that a combined publication of John Hunt and Henning Smidth Olsen will one day appear in a third edition.

Mention must also be made of various books which, though they do not concern Furtwängler directly, deal with aspects of his life at some length. First and foremost is Berta Geissmar's *The Baton and the Jackboot* (London 1944). It is her autobiography, but as she was Furtwängler's secretary between 1922 and 1934, before she worked for Sir Thomas Beecham and the London Philharmonic, it contains vital information about Furtwängler during those crucial years. Then there is Friedrich Herzfeld's *Magie des Taktstocks: Die Welt der grossen Dirigenten, Konzerte und Orchester* (Berlin 1953), a book about conductors in general which devotes no less than fifteen pages to Furtwängler. There are also various booklets about the Leipzig *Gewandhaus* and the Berlin and Vienna Philharmonic Orchestras, in particular Peter Muck's *Einhundert Jahre Berliner Philharmonisches Orchester* (3 vols, Tutzing 1982) which provides much valuable information and documentary evidence. Lastly, there is Fred K. Prieberg's *Musik im NS Staat* (Frankfurt 1982) which has a great deal to say about Furtwängler and other musicians during the Nazi period.

Compositions

At Furtwängler's death all manuscripts in his possession, musical and otherwise, passed into the hands of his widow, Frau Elisabeth Furtwängler. James Ellis went to Clarens and, with the consent and cooperation of Frau Furtwängler, surveyed all Furtwängler's own compositions and compiled a chronological listing. This was published in August 1975 and subsequently reprinted in a Newsletter of the Wilhelm Furtwängler Society (UK). Ellis was also responsible for the list of Furtwängler's compositions in Grove. Later Frau Furtwängler presented the whole literary and musical estate to the *Zentralbibliothek* Zürich, where it is in the keeping of the Music Department headed by Dr Günter Birkner, assisted by Dr Mireille Geering. They kindly supplied me with a provisional catalogue (dated August 1985) based on Ellis. This is in preparation for a complete chronological and thematic catalogue of all Furtwängler's compositions which, of course, will take some time to prepare. The following list, in a condensed form, is a compilation of these two sources.

1.a   *Kompositionen von Willy Furtwängler* (1893-95) vol.1. Collated by his mother. A collection of 26 pieces, some only sketches. 22 for Pf. Solo, 1 for Pf. Duet, 3 songs for Voice & Pf.

1.b   *Verschiedene Compositionen für Klavier von Wilhelm Furtwängler im Alter von 8-9 Jahren* (1894/95). 8 pieces for Pf.

1.c   *Compositionen von Wilhelm Furtwängler* (1895) vol.2. A collection of 16 pieces, some only sketches. 10 for Pf. Solo, 3 for Pf. Duet, 2 for Voice & Pf., 1 for Vocal Duet & Pf.

1.d   *Kleine Melodie*, G major, for Pf. Duet.

1.e   *Stück*, G major, for Pf. Duet: Theme with 2 Variations (1895).

1.f   *Anfang*, D minor, for Pf. (1895).

1.g   *Sonate*, C major, for Pf. (1895).

1.h   *Rondo*, F major, for Pf. (1895?).

Compositions

2.a   *Lieder für Gesang und Klavier* (1895-1900?). 15 songs complete, 3 unfinished.

2.b   *Sonate*, F major, for Vl. & Pf. (1896).

3.   *Sonaten für Klavier* (1896-98). 5 sonatas and 3 other short pieces for Pf.

4.   *Kleine Sonata*, E major, for Vcl. & Pf. (1896).

5.   *Trio*, F major, for Vl., Vcl. & Pf. (1896).

6.   *Quartett quasi una fantasia*, F major, for 2 Vl., Vla. & Vcl. (1896).

7.   *Trio*, C major, for 2 Vl. & Vcl. (1896/97).

8.   *Variationen*, G major, for 2 Vl., Vla. & Vcl. (1897).

9.   *Die erste Walpurgisnacht*, for S-A-B Soli, 2 Choirs & Orch. (1898). A cantata in 17 movements.

10.a   *Fantasie* No.1, D minor, for Pf. (1901?).

10.b   *Fantasie* No.2, C minor, for Pf. (1901).

11.   *Ich wandelte unter den Bäumen*, for S-A Soli, Chorus S-S-A-A & Pf. (1898).

12.a   *Fuga*, E major, for Pf. (1898).

12.b   *Fuga*, B major, for Pf. (1898?).

13.   *Fantasia*, F major, for Pf. Duet (1898).

14.   *Sonate*, A minor, for Vl. & Pf. (1898/99).

15.   *Quartett*, C minor, for Vl., Vla., Vcl. & Pf. (1899).

16.   *Ouvertüre*, E flat major, for Orch. (1899).

17.   *Trio*, E major, for Vl., Vcl. & Pf. (1900).

18.   *Fantasie*, C major, for Vl., Vcl. & Pf. (1900).

19.   *Zwei Fantasien*, G major & C minor, for Pf. (1900).

19.(i)   *Streichquartett*, E minor. No trace of the music, but Furtwängler mentions it in detail in a letter of 27 January 1900.

19.(ii)   *Sextett*. No trace of the music, but Furtwängler mentions it in two letters of 26 June and 20 December 1901.

Compositions

20.   *Quartett*, F sharp minor, for 2 Vl., Vla. & Vcl. (1901?).

21.a   *Kleinigkeiten.* Three pieces for Pf., E major, G major & F major (1902).

21.b   *Drei Klavierstücke*, E major, G major & E major (1903?). The first 2 pieces in Nos. 21.a and 21.b are very similar, in parts identical.

22.a   *Schwindet, ihr dunklen Wölbungen*, for Chorus & Orch. (1902). Text from Goethe's *Faust*, Part I.

22.b   *Scherzo*, G major, for Pf. (1902?).

22.c   *Scherzo*, C major, for Pf. (1902?).

22.d   *Trio*, G major, for Vl., Vcl. & Pf. (1902). Fragmentary.

23.a   *O du Jungfrau, höchste Herrscherin der Welt*, Religious Hymn, for S-T Soli, Chorus & Orch. (1903). Text from Goethe's *Faust*, Part II.

23.b   *Sinfonie*, F sharp minor (1903). Incomplete score of a third movement, possibly belonging to 24.a.

24.a   *Sinfonie*, D major, *Allegro* (1903). Sketchy score of a first movement. It can be conjectured that, together with 23.b, this may form part of the early Symphony performed in Breslau.

24.b   *Festliche Ouvertüre*, F major, for Orch. (1904).

25.   *Sinfonie*, B minor, first movement, *Largo* (1908). Presumably a revision of the *Symphonic Adagio* of 1906.

26.   *Te deum*, for Soli, Chorus & Orch. (1902-09).

27.   *Quintett*, C major, for 2 Vl., Vla., Vcl. & Pf. (1932-35).

28.   *Sonate*, D minor, for Vl. & Pf. (1935). Published 1938 by Breitkopf & Härtel, Leipzig.

29.   *Sinfonisches Konzert*, B minor, for Pf. & Orch. (1937). Published 1954 by Brucknerverlag, Wiesbaden.

30.   *Sonate*, D major, for Vl. & Pf. (1938/39). Published 1940 by Bote & Bock, Berlin.

31.   *Sinfonie Nr.1*, B minor (1938?-41). After a try-out in a rehearsal Furtwängler rejected the work.

32.   *Sinfonie Nr.2*, E minor (1944-45). Published 1952 by Brucknerverlag, Wiesbaden.

Compositions

33.   *Sinfonie Nr.3*, C sharp minor (1952/53). Furtwängler was dissatisfied with the Finale but was prevented by his death from revising it. Study Score published privately (for members only) by the Wilhelm Furtwängler Society, Japan.

The *Zentralbibliothek* Zürich still holds many sketches which they have not yet been able to examine in detail, and it is possible that the items 19.(i) and 19.(ii) may be found among them.

Chronology

The following abbreviations are used:

BPO	Berlin Philharmonic Orchestra
LPO	London Philharmonic Orchestra
LSO	London Symphony Orchestra
VPO	Vienna Philharmonic Orchestra

1853	30 Jun: Adolf Furtwängler (father) born.
1863	14 Sep: Adelheid Wendt (mother) born.
1886	25 Jan: Wilhelm Furtwängler born in Berlin.
1893	First youthful compositions.
1894	Appointment of Adolf Furtwängler to Munich University. Family moves to Munich.
1896	High School studies. Piano lessons and lessons in theory and composition. Taken out of school about two years later and entrusted to Curtius and Riezler for private tuition. Acquisition of country house *Tanneck* on the Tegernsee.
1901	Visit to Greece, where his father is engaged on archaeological work.
1902	In Florence with Curtius. Friendship with the Hildebrand family. Studies with Max von Schillings.
1903	Piano tuition by Conrad Ansorge, Berlin.
1903–04	Composition of early Symphony in D major, first performed in Breslau.
1905–06	Repetiteur at the Breslau Municipal Theatre.
1906	Conducts first orchestral concert in Munich, including an *Adagio* of his own and Bruckner IX.
1906–07	Repetiteur and Assistant Conductor at the Zürich Municipal Theatre.
1907	10 Oct: Father's death in Athens.
1907–09	Repetiteur at the Munich Court Opera under Felix Mottl.
1909–11	Third Conductor at the Strasbourg Opera under Hans Pfitzner.
1910	Nov: First performance of his *Te Deum* in Breslau under Georg Dohrn.
1911–15	Chief Conductor of the Lübeck Symphony Orchestra in succession to Hermann Abendroth. Guest appearances at the Lübeck Opera (*Fidelio, Meistersinger*, etc.).
1912	Feb: First meeting with Arthur Nikisch in Hamburg.

Chronology

1913	Apr: Conducts Beethoven IX for the first time.
	Jun: First guest appearance in Vienna.
1915–20	*Hofkapellmeister* in Mannheim in succession to Arthur Bodansky.
1917	14 Dec: First guest appearance in Berlin with BPO.
1918–19	Guest appearances at the Frankfurt *Museumskonzerte*.
1919	On the retirement of Ferdinand Loewe becomes Conductor of the regular concerts of the *Tonkünstler-Orchester* in Vienna (until 1924).
1920	2 Apr: Guest engagement with the orchestra of the Berlin State Opera. Appointed Conductor of that orchestra in 1920 as successor to Richard Strauss.
	Aug: Takes over the Frankfurt *Museumskonzerte* in succession to Willem Mengelberg.
1921	First appearances as guest conductor with the Leipzig *Gewandhaus* Orchestra.
1922	23 Jan: Death of Arthur Nikisch. Furtwängler subsequently becomes his successor as Conductor of the *Gewandhaus* Orchestra (until 1928) and the BPO.
	3 Apr: First concert with VPO in Vienna.
1923	22 May: Marries Zitla Lund.
	Winter: Purchase of the holiday chalet near St Moritz.
1924	Jan/Feb: First appearances as guest conductor in London. 4 concerts, 2 with the orchestra of the Royal Philharmonic Society, 2 with the LSO.
	Autumn: First concert tour with BPO through Germany and Switzerland.
1925	Jan: First visit to America. 10 concerts in New York with the New York Philharmonic.
1926	Feb-Apr: Second visit to America. 32 concerts with the New York Philharmonic (26 in New York, 2 in Pittsburgh, 1 each in Philadelphia, Washington, Baltimore, Reading).
1927	Feb-Apr: Third visit to America. 33 concerts with the New York Philharmonic (27 in New York, 2 in Pittsburgh, 1 each in Philadelphia, Washington, Baltimore, Harrisburg).
	Jun: Beethoven Festival. Receives an Honorary Doctorate from Heidelberg University.
	Autumn: Appointed Chief Conductor of VPO in succession to Felix Weingartner (until 1930).
	Dec: First tour to England with BPO (2 concerts in London, 1 in Manchester).
1928	Spring: First visit to Paris with BPO.
	17 Oct: First appearance as guest conductor at the Vienna Opera (*Rheingold*).
	Autumn: Appointed 'Municipal General Music Director' of Berlin. Refuses to take over the direction of the Vienna Opera.
	Nov: 4 concerts with BPO in London and Liverpool. Visits to England now virtually become annual events until 1938.
1929	May: Elected to the *Friedensklasse des Pour le mérite*.
1930	April: First concert tour with VPO to England (2 concerts).
1931	Accepts overall musical direction of Bayreuth Festival. Three per-

formances of *Tristan*.

1931–32   First tour of Italy with BPO.

1932   7 Jun: First appearance as guest conductor at the Paris *Opéra* (*Tristan*); then almost every year until 1938.

Awarded the Goethe Medal.

1933   30 Jan: Hitler comes to power.

12 Apr: Open letter to Goebbels in defence of Jewish artists.

Jun: Appointed Chief Conductor of the Berlin State Opera.

Jul: Göring appoints him *Staatsrat*.

Aug: Confrontation with Hitler on the Obersalzberg.

1934   25 Nov: Publication of a newspaper article '*Der Fall Hindemith*' leads to his resignation from all official posts. Confiscation of his passport.

1935   Mar: Compromise reached with Goebbels; no official posts, but prepared to work as guest conductor in Germany.

20 & 24 May: First guest appearances, Royal Opera House Covent Garden, London (*Tristan*).

Completion of his Piano Quintet in C major.

1936   Feb/Mar: Holiday in Egypt with John Knittel.

Smear campaign against him in America. Cancellation of plans to become Toscanini's successor with New York Philharmonic.

Summer: Bayreuth Festival (*Parsifal, Lohengrin, Der Ring des Nibelungen*). Meeting with Sir Thomas Beecham.

1936–37   Sep-Feb: Takes sabbatical from conducting and concentrates on composition.

1937   Mar: First performance of his Violin Sonata No.1 in D minor.

25 Mar: Performance of Beethoven IX in London with LPO and Philharmonic Choir.

May: Coronation Season of King George VI. Conducts 2 concerts with BPO in London and 2 *Ring* cycles at Covent Garden.

Summer: Bayreuth Festival (*Parsifal, Ring*).

27 Aug: First appearance at Salzburg Festival (Beethoven IX).

Sep: 'German Week' at World Fair in Paris (Beethoven IX, *Walküre*).

Oct: First performance of his Symphonic Concerto for Piano and Orchestra, Munich, with Edwin Fischer.

1938   Jan: Last tour of England before the war with BPO.

13 Mar: Hitler annexes Austria.

May/Jun: Last appearances as guest conductor at Covent Garden, London (2 *Ring* cycles).

21 Jun: Conducts 100th performance of *Tristan* at Paris *Opéra*.

Aug: First appearances at Salzburg Festival as opera conductor (*Meistersinger*).

27 Dec: Last appearance at Paris *Opéra* (*Siegfried*).

1939   Jun: Resumes Musical Directorship of VPO.

Jul: Appointed *Commandeur de la Légion d'Honneur* by the French Government (*Décret* of 10 Jan 1939).

3 Sep: Outbreak of Second World War.

1940   Feb: First performance of his Violin Sonata No.2 in D major.

1941   Mar: Skiing accident; prevented from all conducting activity until Oct.

1942   Jun: Tour of Switzerland with BPO.

Chronology

1943	May: Tour of Scandinavia with VPO.
	26 Jun: Marries Elisabeth Ackermann *née* Albert.
	Summer: Bayreuth Festival (*Meistersinger*).
1944	12 Jan: His last concert in the old Berlin *Philharmonie*.
	30 Jan: Total destruction of Berlin *Philharmonie* in an air raid.
	Summer: Conducts opera for the last time in Bayreuth (*Meistersinger*).
	Aug/Sep: First appearance at Lucerne Festival.
	Nov: Mother dies in Heidelberg.
	11 Nov: Son Andreas born in Switzerland.
1945	23 Jan: Last concert (until 1947) with BPO in Berlin.
	28 Jan: Last concert (until 1947) with VPO in Vienna.
	7 Feb: Escapes to Switzerland.
	12 & 14 Feb: Concerts in Geneva and Lausanne.
	20 Feb: A concert in Zürich banned by local authorities owing to anti-German feeling.
	23 Feb: Conducts in Winterthur. His last concert until 1947.
	Mar: Dr Paul Niehans offers him a home at his clinic *La Prairie* in Clarens near Montreux.
1944–45	Composition of Symphony No.2. First sketches of Symphony No.3.
1946	Spring: First meeting with Menuhin.
	Dec: Denazification proceedings in Berlin.
1947	Jan: Cleared of all charges by Allied tribunal. Ratification delayed until May (?).
	Takes up residence with family in *Villa l'Empéreur* (Clarens). Granted permanent residence in Switzerland.
	6-9 Apr: Concerts in Rome and Florence.
	25 May: First concert in Berlin with BPO since end of war.
	10-13 Aug: Salzburg Festival.
	20-30 Aug: Lucerne Festival.
	Oct: Guest conductor in Stockholm.
	21 & 31 Oct: Conducts again at Berlin State Opera (*Tristan*).
1948	24/25 Jan: 2 concerts in Paris with *Orchestre du Conservatoire*.
	22 Feb: First performance of his Symphony No.2, Berlin.
	Feb/Mar: First post-war visit to England (10 concerts with LPO).
	Apr/May: Visit to Buenos Aires (8 concerts).
	Jul/Aug: Salzburg Festival.
	Aug: Lucerne Festival.
	Sep: Edinburgh Festival; 2 concerts with St Cecilia Orchestra of Rome.
	Sep/Oct: Tour to England with VPO (5 concerts).
	Nov: Tour to England with BPO (4 concerts).
1948–49	Invited to Chicago but invitation revoked because of another campaign of hatred.
1949	Tours all over Europe, either as guest or with his own orchestras.
	Jul/Aug: Salzburg Festival.
	Aug: Lucerne Festival.
	Sep: Besançon Festival with Paris *Colonne* Orchestra.
	Sep/Oct: Tour of England with VPO, followed by concerts in Paris and Switzerland.

1950   Mar/Apr: 3 *Ring* cycles at *La Scala*, Milan.
Apr/May: 10 concerts in Buenos Aires.
22 May: First guest appearance in London with the Philharmonia Orchestra.
Jul/Aug: Salzburg Festival.
Aug: Lucerne Festival.
Sep/Oct: Tour of Scandinavia, Germany and Switzerland with VPO.

1951   Apr: 10 concerts in Egypt with BPO.
29 Jul: Conducts Beethoven IX at reinauguration of Bayreuth Festival.
Aug: Salzburg and Lucerne Festivals, *Zürcher Festwochen*.

1952   Jun: Recording of *Tristan und Isolde* with London Philharmonia Orchestra.
Jul: Breakdown during rehearsals at Salzburg. Period of severe illness.

1953   Jan/Feb: Tours through Germany with BPO.
22 Apr: Last concert in London with BPO.
Jul/Aug: Salzburg Festival. Accompanies Schwarzkopf in a Hugo Wolf Recital.
Aug: Lucerne Festival.
Sep: Edinburgh Festival: 4 concerts with VPO.
Oct/Nov: Recording for *Radio Italiana* of the *Ring*.

1954   12 Mar: Last appearance in London with Philharmonia Orchestra (Festival Hall).
Mar: 2 concerts in Caracas with the Symphony Orchestra of Venezuela.
May: Last concerts in Paris (with BPO).
Summer: Acquisition of *Villa Basset Coulon* in Clarens, his home for the last few months of his life.
Jul/Aug: Salzburg Festival.
9 Aug: Beethoven IX in Bayreuth.
Aug: Lucerne Festival with Philharmonia Orchestra.
6 Sep: Beethoven Concert at Besançon Festival with *Orchestre de la Radiodiffusion Française*.
20 Sep: Last concert with BPO, Berlin. Programme includes his own Symphony No.2.
Sep/Oct: Studio recording of *Walküre* in Vienna.
5-12 Nov: Clarens. Work on Symphony No.3.
12 Nov: Seriously ill; transfer to clinic Ebersteinburg near Baden-Baden.
30 Nov: Wilhelm Furtwängler dies.

Index

179

Index